THE
MID-EAST
PEACE
PUZZLE

THE
MID-EAST
PEACE
PUZZLE

HILTON SUTTON
with
ZOLA LEVITT

THOMAS NELSON PUBLISHERS
Nashville • Camden • New York

Published in Nashville, Tennessee, by Thomas Nelson, Inc. and distributed in Canada by Lawson Falle, Ltd., Cambridge, Ontario.

Printed in the United States of America.

Seventh Printing

Library of Congress Cataloging in Publication Data

Sutton, Hilton.
    The Mid-east peace puzzle.

    1. Bible—Prophecies—Palestine.
2. Jewish-Arab relations.   I.   Levitt, Zola.
II.   Title.
BS649.P3S87   220.1′5   79-19234
ISBN 0-8407-5703-4

CONTENTS

INTRODUCTION

Hilton Sutton is a tireless student of prophecy and a particularly sharp-eyed observer of current events. He has a unique and stirring way of comparing the political scenes of today with passages of the Bible. His various publications, tape recordings, and sermons are valued highly by biblically aware Christians, and his cogent analyses of the world scene have drawn the interest of many unbelievers as well.

The source of this book is an urgent sermon delivered to a church of biblically taught believers. The text is adapted from the tape, called *Pharaoh In the Promised Land,* available from Mission to America Tapes, 736 Wilson Road, Humble, Texas 77338. I urge you to obtain this tape and the other Sutton tapes; mere writing—"cold type," as it is referred to—cannot begin to express the enthusiasm, energy, and urgency of Hilton Sutton's teaching.

This evangelist is what Christians refer to as an "anointed" speaker. His messages are full of emphatic appeals to his listeners to take action on the will of God, stimulating digressions on many books of the Bible, and a touch of ironic humor. I hope that the writing in this book will bring out these intangible factors while presenting important factual information.

Without a doubt, the subject is important. Hilton Sutton delivered this message in early January, 1978, a few weeks after the historic meeting of President Sadat of Egypt and Prime Minister Begin of Israel. Sutton recognized the great importance of the peace processes following this momentous meeting, although his conclusions may surprise some. His sermon discussed the peace efforts of the two leaders and the ominous interest of Russia, with reference to the prophecies of Ezekiel and Paul.

Sutton then made a verbal study of the leading characters in the drama, including President Carter, and developed the intriguing biblical background of the relationship between Israel and Egypt. He reviewed with frightening clarity the coming Russian invasion of Israel and its scriptural sanctions, and concluded his talk with joyous reference to the Rapture of the church and the second coming of our King.

If this book has an overall message, it is simply this: The stage is set, the end is near, the prophets have spoken, and God is very much in charge.

INTRODUCTION

Events are taking shape today in such a way as to inspire the informed body of Christ to rejoice, to labor with renewed zeal, and to look to the kingdom of heaven, which is very much at hand.

Very relevant to the message that follows is the brief introduction from the tape, *Pharaoh in the Promised Land:*

Today's newspapers are filled with stories from the Middle East. The same headlines you read daily can be read in the Scriptures. Every major Middle East event has been recorded in God's Word, and with a knowledge of these prophetic Scriptures we can be looking for signs to follow. Among the leading authorities on Bible prophecy and current events is Hilton Sutton. Listen now as God's timetable is brought up to date in mid-January, 1978.

—Zola Levitt

THE
MID-EAST
PEACE
PUZZLE

1

SUDDEN DESTRUCTION

We have all been patiently watching as the powers of the Middle East try to find the right combination for peace. The remarkable events of November, 1977, have forever changed the complexion of this part of the world, and it appears now that we may reasonably look forward to at least a temporary time of peace.

This particular time of peace was prophesied a long time ago in the Bible. We may refer immediately to three vital biblical verses:

After many days thou shalt be visited: in the latter years thou shalt come into the land that is brought back from the sword, and is gathered out of many people, against the mountains of Israel, which have been always waste:

but it is brought forth out of the nations, *and they shall dwell safely all of them*. ... And thou shalt say, I will go up to the land of unwalled villages; *I will go to them that are at rest, that dwell safely , all of them dwelling without walls, and having neither bars nor gates*. ... Therefore, son of man, prophesy and say unto Gog, Thus saith the Lord GOD; *In that day when my people of Israel dwelleth safely*, shalt thou not know it? (Ezek. 38:8,11,14, italics mine).

The prophet Ezekiel emphasizes a future peacetime for the restored nation of Israel. Ezekiel's prophecies were written nearly 2,600 years ago; but the chapter in question, coming as it does after the prophet's remarkable "vision of the dry bones," must refer to *restored* Israel—that is, Israel after A.D. 1948. In Ezekiel 37, the prophet made clear that someday there would be an Israel that the Lord would gather from the tribes scattered throughout the world. We saw in Ezekiel 38:8 that the prophet refers to an Israel "brought forth out of the nations," and it is clear that this Israel is the one we see today.

In the long period from the writings of Ezekiel to the dispersion of the Jews in the first and second centuries A.D., there was no time of peace for Israel. The Promised Land suffered under the yoke of constant domination by foreign powers.

The whole world is now watching a thirty-one-year-old nation that has not enjoyed a day of peace since its inception. Israel was reborn in 1948 in a bloody war for independence and has remained steadily mobilized or actually at war ever since. Four terrifying wars have raged in the Holy Land since Israel's declaration of independence: the initial battle of 1948; the combined Arab assault of 1956; the amazing Six-Day War of 1967 (in which the Jewish people recovered their ancient capital, Jerusalem, and the site of the temples); and the devastating Yom Kippur War of 1973, in which it seemed momentarily that Israel might finally be annihilated.

Indeed, we have yet to see the idyllic time of peace spoken of by Ezekiel.

"Let Us Not Sleep"

If that's all there was in prophecy, then Israel could look forward to a time of uninterrupted peace and rest. But the prophet Ezekiel could see further than that, and so could the apostle Paul. Paul put it succinctly:

For when they shall say, Peace and safety; then sudden destruction cometh upon them, as travail upon a woman with child (1 Thess. 5:3).

Thus this great apostle likened this "sudden destruction" to the pain of labor in childbirth. It will come suddenly, following a period of relative comfort and rest. Just as surely as a woman expecting a child will go suddenly into "travail," so the world, enjoying what is presumed to be "peace and safety," will suddenly see devastating war.

Paul then continued with a message we Christians might well heed as we carefully study these end-time events:

But ye, brethren, are not in darkness, that that day should overtake you as a thief. Ye are all the children of light, and the children of the day: we are not of the night, nor of darkness. Therefore, let us not sleep, as do others; but let us watch and be sober (1 Thess. 5:4—6).

Ezekiel 38 and 39 detail a great invasion by a northern power which will put an end to this time of peace. We are able to pinpoint this power geographically by Ezekiel's references to the "far north" or "uttermost north" (38:15, 39:2, accurately translated). A line drawn due north from Jerusalem on a world globe *will pass through Moscow.* Previous biblical commentators, even without the advantage of seeing current developments, had nevertheless identified Russia as the invader called "Magog" by Ezekiel. The original Scofield Bible (copyright 1907) and other informed sources concurred—even before the restoration of Israel and the rise of Russia to world importance.

The temporary peace noted by the prophets will act only as a signal for Russia to invade. When all are relaxed and "at rest," when the world at last breathes easily about the Middle Eastern situation, then Russia will make her lightning thrust into the Middle East.

We have an obvious advantage over Bible readers of the past who tried to work out the visions of Ezekiel. We take it for granted today that Russia is a dangerous expansionist power in the Eastern Hemisphere, and we have seen her occupy land after land by means of sudden invasion. Even ten years ago it would have been difficult for any political analyst to foresee an invasion of Israel by

Russia; twenty years ago it would have seemed extremely unlikely; and thirty years ago it would have been simply impossible, since Russia recognized the new State of Israel in 1948 by voting to accept her delegation to the United Nations.

But five years ago the picture became clearer as the world saw Russia arm the combined Arab enemies of Israel with the most sophisticated weaponry and technical assistance of that time. And today, even for those with no familiarity with the Bible, Russia's intentions are easy to discern. Would any of us be honestly surprised to see Russia invade Israel?

Ezekiel, considered a fool in his time and perhaps the most obtuse of all prophets of the Bible, is rapidly coming into fashion. His book appears to have been written this year.

The African Connection

We need not merely theorize that Russia will invade Israel because she has invaded many other nations. Ezekiel was more precise than that, and we can be also if we understand the prophet.

A recent news article described the Arabs' plea to the United States to speak strongly to Russia about her involvement in Africa, particularly in Ethiopia. It's certainly no secret to those interested in Russian politics that the Communists, having already controlled parts of the Orient so effectively, intend to take a foothold wherever they can in Africa. Most of Asia has fallen to Communism, and so has a good part of Europe. Africa and the Middle East remain as prizes for Communist expansion, and the Red flag already flies in many places on the Dark Continent.

The Arabs are concerned about Russian influence in Ethiopia because they fear an Ethiopian invasion of neighboring Somaliland. However, Ezekiel takes the longer view, listing Ethiopia as one of Russia's allies in the coming invasion of Israel (Ezek. 38:5).

The United States is also interested in preventing Russian expansion. Americans fear the time when Russia will dominate such numbers of people and such vast stretches of territory that they become a threat to the entire Western world.

Somaliland is a small place, quite out of the way in the comings and goings of the major powers, but so was Korea and Viet Nam. The Arabs do not want to see the mighty Communist war machine so close to their own borders, although they have gladly accepted Russia's assistance in the past when Israel was the intended victim.

The progress of Russia in Africa and the presence of so many Communist-inspired insurrections and wars have disconcerted free people everywhere. When the *Arabs* begin to sit up and take notice, it's certainly time for real concern!

Through the African connection, Russia will gain a new ally, Ethiopia. Libya is another African country that will ally itself with Russia because of its unflinching hatred of Israel.

Future Shock

Much of the Word of God is coming to pass today; what was once a jigsaw puzzle of prophetic pieces is beginning to coalesce into an overall picture. The future is becoming clear enough that we can project its events, with the help and guidance of the Scriptures.

It is not a bright future, but the church must take it into consideration in its worldly assignment. We must not be shocked or frightened in any way. In fact, we rejoice—even amidst the travail that must fall upon the unbeliever—in the sure knowledge that the coming of our King will follow. These are not days in which the church must shudder or be fearful, or even be perplexed. Rather, these days should inspire us to greater efforts as God brings His ultimate plan to fruition. We can understand that plan because we have this magnificent Book, this accurate Book of future events, to utilize in comprehending this extremely complicated world around us.

A reasonable prediction is that this present peace program will surge ahead and then pause, and then surge ahead still again, but pause again. And if we wonder just how it is that the leaders cannot sit down together and make peace, let us realize one thing: God is sovereign and He is in charge. He has a schedule and a plan. We are seeing opposition to peace by Arab powers at the present time, but this is merely a sign of God's sovereignty. We can be certain that the prophets are accurate and that real peace will ensue, and

even that the presently hostile Arabs will participate in it. That will be the outcome on God's
timetable, however men appear to arrive at it. God
is by no means leaving it up to man to push the
right button, turn the right wheel, or pull the right
lever these days. We can be assured that He is
operating the mechanisms that will lead first to
peace and ultimately to war—and, after all is
finished, to the establishment of His kingdom.

We can look back to times when there didn't
seem to be many prophetic fulfillments; even those
who read the Bible wondered if men, not God,
were running this world. But we need not question
that at a time like this. With the restoration of Israel in 1948, a huge piece of the prophetic puzzle
fell into place, and now many other pieces seem to
fit into the scheme.

Again we stress that the actions are not
man's—they are God's. There should be no "future
shock" for the church, although a best seller by
that peculiar title theorized that the future is arriv-
ing so fast that it is shocking. Paul warned us
there would be no shock as we saw events trans-
pire exactly as they were foretold for us. He only
admonished, "Let us watch." As we go on with this
prophetic analysis, let us indeed watch with great
care, keeping our minds open to God's Holy Word.

We turn now to the leading characters in the
drama, the leaders of what have recently become
the most important nations in today's world.

2

THE SOVEREIGNTY OF GOD

In 1976, God made a stunningly significant move in His plan for the end of this age.

Let us digress for a moment to consider the sovereignty of God and certain elements of His character as they are expressed in the Bible. God is in a relationship with men, and faithful men have achieved real friendship with Him. We can come to the point where He will actually "talk things over" with us. Remember the story of God and Abraham, "the friend of God." God had announced the imminent destruction of the cities of Sodom and Gomorrah, where Abraham's nephew Lot lived. Abraham sought to intercede with God for the sake of the righteous few who might be found within those cities:

And Abraham drew near and said, Wilt thou also destroy the righteous with the wicked? Peradventure there be fifty righteous within the city: wilt thou also destroy and not spare the place for the fifty righteous that are therein? (Gen. 18:23,24).

We might tremble at the thought of a man interrogating the God of heaven and earth about His plans, but Abraham presumed to argue that righteous men—even if there were only fifty to be found in those two large cities—should not be destroyed.

God replied amicably enough:

And the Lord said, If I find in Sodom fifty righteous within the city, then I will spare all the place for their sakes (Gen. 18:26).

Having made some headway, Abraham petitioned again and God answered once more in the positive:

Peradventure there shall lack five of the fifty righteous: wilt thou destroy all the city for lack of five? And he said, If I find there forty and five, I will not destroy it (Gen. 18:28).

And amazingly enough, Abraham continued to talk with God until he arrived at the figure of ten righteous men:

And he said, Oh let not the Lord be angry, and I will speak yet but this once: Peradventure ten shall be found there. And he said, I will not destroy it for ten's sake (Gen. 18:32).

22

Actually, this was wasted effort. We find later on that there were not even ten righteous men in those wicked cities. But the story nevertheless shows how men may commune with God and how reasonable God is, even to the point of "bargaining."

If we carefully observe God's will and His movements, we too can commune with Him. God is not sovereign in the sense that He is a harsh judge or taskmaster. He is omnipotent, it is true, but every believer can communicate with Him, and He is a considerate and loving God.

The Seventh President

At the beginning of the chapter, 1976 was described as a special year. In that year, God in His wisdom chose to place at the head of our mighty nation a man who would set in motion the remarkable events we are seeing now in the Middle East. Jimmy Carter is president of the United States by the divine will of God. We realize from the Scriptures that leaders occupy their positions by divine appointment: "But God is the judge: he putteth down one, and setteth up another" (Ps. 75:7).

In Daniel 5 we find a more explicit example of God's sovereignty over the high offices of men. Daniel was explaining to Belshazzar the meaning of the handwriting on the wall and the fate of Nebuchadnezzar. Daniel said, in effect, "Belshazzar, one thing Nebuchadnezzar learned that you have chosen to overlook is that God reigns over all and

God selects whom He will to reign over the nations of men."

It is perfectly reasonable to assume that there is no national leader anywhere whom God has not chosen to occupy his particular position. Obviously, there are vile and wicked men occupying government positions around the world, but they are still the choice of God. Whether by the demands of their own people or because they will advance God's ultimate plans, these men rule by the will of God.

In any case, our current president told us in his campaign that he was a vigorous supporter of Israel. He claimed he understood the prophetic position of that singular nation. Even as a candidate, Carter seemed to appreciate Israel's great destiny in world affairs. As president, he also proclaimed publicly that he was born again. Never before in our history has a president made such a point of his relationship with God. Furthermore, Israel was quite an issue in the campaign for the presidency; Carter won that office by a narrow margin. He drew quite a few votes from the Christian church because of his stand toward God and prophecy.

Jimmy Carter, upon his election, became the *seventh* president of the United States in the time of restored Israel. In the Bible, the number seven indicates completion. God made the world in seven days and He chose to have seven lamps in the tabernacle, seven feasts for Israel, seven churches in Asia, and so forth.

Israel was restored under President Harry Truman. Then followed the presidencies of Dwight

Eisenhower, John F. Kennedy, Lyndon Johnson, Richard Nixon, Gerald Ford, and Jimmy Carter.

The six presidents who preceded Carter gave their complete support to the nation of Israel, and our nation has been abundantly blessed during that period of time and under those presidents.

England also had the opportunity to receive many blessings. Great Britain, through General Allenby in 1917 (during World War I), took the Holy Land from the Turks. At that time, Lord Balfour went before the British Parliament and succeeded in getting the Parliament to partition off an area within the Holy Land and give it back to the Jews. This proposal was called the Balfour Agreement.

But Britain, after taking over the Holy Land, partitioning out parts of that land, and legally giving it back to the Jews, was to become the very nation that would aid in *opposing* the Jews when the time came for them to take advantage of that legal document and go home. After World War II, when the Jews began to return to the land of their fathers as outlined in the Balfour Agreement, Great Britain opposed them with imprisonment and bullets!

Menachem Begin had the British headquarters in Jerusalem bombed on a number of occasions, and the British put a price on his head! It surprises many people to realize that Begin, the distinguished prime minister of Israel, was once wanted dead or alive by the British. As a freedom fighter during Israel's difficult struggle for independence, Begin proved himself a great guerrilla commander.

Conceivably, Britain could have had the kind of blessings America now enjoys. God made Himself most plain to His friend Abraham: "And I will bless them that bless thee, and curse him that curseth thee: and in thee shall all families of the earth be blessed" (Gen. 12:3).

Obviously, the United States ought not to change its position of friendship toward Israel. But there seems little danger of that at present, considering that President Carter so energetically pursues a policy of peace in the Middle East. It can fairly be said that President Carter is the first of the American presidents since 1948 to adamantly *insist* on a Middle East peace.

Carter is headed in a biblical direction. If we look into Isaiah 19—the definitive chapter on Egypt—we can see a marvelous prophecy of peace in the Middle East:

In that day shall there be a highway out of Egypt to Assyria, and the Assyrians shall come into Egypt, and the Egyptians into Assyria, and the Egyptians shall serve with the Assyrians. In that day shall Israel be the third with Egypt and with Assyria, even a blessing in the midst of the land: Whom the Lord of hosts shall bless, saying, Blessed be Egypt my people, and Assyria the work of my hands, and Israel mine inheritance (Isa. 19:23—25).

So we have it on the good authority of Isaiah, the dean of the Old Testament prophets, that there will eventually be perfect peace in the Middle East. Syria (ancient Assyria actually covered somewhat more territory than modern Syria), Israel, and Egypt will someday achieve a level of harmony in which the Lord will bless all three nations and give each one a special and loving title. Considering the present-day relationship between Israel and those two major Arab antagonists, Isaiah's prophecy is a most encouraging one.

The Unlikely Prime Minister

If we can surmise that God placed Jimmy Carter in office, we can certainly assume no less of Prime Minister Begin. In fact, in the case of Begin, the hand of God has moved perhaps even more clearly. By all logical reckoning, Begin was a very unlikely candidate for the highest office in Israel's government.

First of all, it is something of a miracle that he is alive at all. Casualties were heavy among the Jews who opposed the British in Israel's restoration years. God brought him through not only alive, but free. Had they managed to catch up with Begin, the British would certainly have imprisoned or executed him. Indeed, merciful acts of God have followed the heroic footsteps of Menachem Begin since his early adulthood.

Not long ago, Israel's government was under the adequate leadership of Yitzhak Rabin. General Rabin had distinguished himself in the 1967 Sinai campaign and seemed an able prime minister of his nation.

Rabin came into power as a result of the fall of Golda Meir's administration, following the 1973 war. The people of Israel became disenchanted with the government of Mrs. Meir because of the near disaster of that war, which came upon the country by surprise. Rabin, with his extensive military experience, was a reasonable choice to succeed Mrs. Meir. And indeed, Rabin seemed to be doing well; there was little doubt that he would win the next general election in Israel and achieve a still greater vote of confidence.

However, it now appears that God took a hand in things. In the spring of 1976, it was discovered that the wife of the prime minister was overdrawn at her bank. This wouldn't be an overly serious matter for any one of us, even if married to the leader of a nation. But these post-Watergate days have affected democracies everywhere, so that many voters have become sensitive to the slightest irregularities in their governments. Still it appeared, at least at first, that Mrs. Rabin had committed no greater sin than failing to balance her checkbook. Then it came to light that she had other bank accounts. She was far from broke.

Mrs. Rabin had broken a kind of national trust. The Israeli people seriously frown on their citizens keeping money outside their own land. Israel is an expensive country to run since it is always on a war footing; money taken out of the economy and placed elsewhere in the world represents a kind of disloyalty. Mrs. Rabin's banking practices raised some eyebrows, to say the least.

Embarrassed, Rabin resigned his post. This was not considered to be the end of Yitzhak Rabin, however, since Israeli politics provided for a general election. The Labor Party, which Rabin led, was certain that the people of Israel would realize that no crime had been committed and would reinstate the former prime minister. They hoped the whole exercise might in fact enhance Rabin's position, since he had been forthright enough to resign and leave his fate in the hands of the voters. He had been sincere with his people and it was felt that they would now rally behind him.

But when the general election was held, the unlikely office-seeker Menachem Begin stepped forward. He was the leader of one of the smallest political groups in all Israel. Seasoned Israeli government watchers felt Begin was wasting his time running for the high office of prime minister.

Apart from his weak backing, Begin had several other strikes against him. He was a right-winger, similar in image to Barry Goldwater in the 1964 American presidential election. He was an extreme conservative, a patriot of the first order who would fall into the class of America's Patrick Henry, George Washington, or Stonewall Jackson. This patriotic nature might have led voters to think he would be extremely radical in conducting Israel's affairs. The majority of the Israelis, it was felt, preferred a middle-ground candidate. The last thing they needed, the experts reckoned, was an undiplomatic zealot. Did Israel, in its tenuous position, really need that kind of leadership? Begin seemed to be too much of a good thing.

On top of all those difficulties, Begin was devoutly religious. The restored Israel had never had a leader so religious as Begin. The modern father of Israel, David Ben Gurion, was a God-fearing man, but he did not share Begin's orthodoxy. From Ben Gurion to Begin, all the prime ministers were less than religiously devoted although they were skillful in politically ruling largely secular Israel.

As the election day drew nearer, Begin gained ground contrary to the expectations of experienced government observers. The experts started to feel that although there was no chance of his being elected, Begin would give Rabin a very good contest. He had an inspiring way about him, and things he said about the Promised Land hit home in heartfelt ways with many Israeli voters. Begin persisted, leaving no doubt where his loyalties lay with regard to his country and to God, and his campaign gained momentum. People were enthused by the former freedom fighter and a deep admiration developed in his camp.

When election day was over, Begin had beaten Rabin and had the privilege of forming a new Israeli government.

In Israeli politics, winning an election and becoming prime minister are different things. The election winner gains the right to form a government and present it to the Knesset, the ruling body of Israel. The 120-member Knesset, roughly comparable to the U.S. Senate, would have to approve that government before the winner could actually take the office of prime minister.

The skeptical political observers predicted the impossibility of this task for Begin. He was, after all, merely a minority leader, a right-winger with many counts against him. For a while it seemed that Begin would not have enough supporters to form a government that would impress the Knesset.

What the political experts had failed to note all along was that Mr. Begin is a shrewd political maneuverer. The patriot Begin faced strong political opponents and somehow convinced them, one by one, that what he had in mind for the leadership of Israel was what Israel needed. Slowly, Begin's former opposition began to join his team. Carefully, almost miraculously, the prime minister-elect was forming a government. In the end, he formed a strong cabinet to offer the Knesset.

Begin fooled the experts again. He gathered a greater majority in the Knesset than anyone had supposed he could. He became prime minister with a position of considerable strength.

From that time until the present, Begin has somehow gained the favor even of his enemies: two of his three most outspoken opponents have now joined his cause. The "experts" at last were silenced and Menachem Begin has become an inspiring and popular prime minister.

The Peace-loving Pharaoh

In the fall of 1977, it all began to happen. Anwar Sadat, the president of Egypt, the modern-day Pharaoh, announced to the world that if invited he would be willing to go to Jerusalem. He would be willing to meet with Prime Minister Begin and address the Israeli Knesset. Sadat indicated that his initial inspiration for such a mission simply "came upon me." He had been in correspondence, it came out, with President Carter.

Was this another move of the Almighty toward peace in the Middle East?

Amazingly enough, this extremely complex issue took less than two weeks to resolve. In fact, in a mere twelve days the invitation was issued by Israel and President Sadat responded and arrived in Jerusalem. By normal diplomatic channels—let us say, by the measure of the relationship between the United States and Russia—such a meeting might have taken months or even years to prepare. Begin and Sadat had worked a mighty miracle. It had been thousands of years since Pharaoh had come to Jerusalem.

Israel and Egypt were the very personification of bad neighbors; they had few dealings with each other, despite their proximity, over an extremely lengthy period of history. There was fighting in Bible times, and very little trade or peacetime interaction.

It must also be understood that Begin could not invite Sadat to Israel as one might ask a neighbor to come over for tea. The prime minister had to approach the Knesset, putting his painstakingly formed government on the line. Here was a great test; here was a vote of confidence over an issue of the utmost importance. Begin could hardly have thought of anything more shocking to put before the Knesset than a suggestion to entertain a man who had sworn to destroy Israel, and from all outward appearances and past performance, was an archenemy of the State of Israel.

Begin was successful at the Knesset, of course, although he did not achieve complete unanimity.

The Communist bloc, a handful of legislators, voted against the idea, as one might well expect. But the invitation was sent and Pharaoh, this time flying in an airplane rather than riding in a chariot, safely crossed the Red Sea.

President Sadat was warmly received at Ben Gurion Airport. The people welcomed him as if he were a hero of Israel. It was a most remarkable scene, appreciated on television around the world.

The meeting between Begin and Sadat was warm and friendly beyond the expectations of most observers. The former enemies shared not the slightest hint of wariness or hostility but instead created what looked like a reunion of brothers.

We are reminded of the story of Jacob and Esau in the Book of Genesis, to which the Begin-Sadat relationship has been compared in some accounts.

In the following chapter we will trace the difficult background of some 4,000 years leading up to the historic and unprecedented meeting of the president of Egypt and the prime minister of Israel.

3

"IT IS WRITTEN"

Middle Eastern arguments and reconciliations go back to the days of the Book of Genesis. We of the modern western nations are often not properly respectful of those whose history reaches back so far. The United States became 200 years old recently; the rivalry between Israel and Egypt started in the time of Abraham, some 4000 years ago!

Abraham's problems began in earnest when he accepted his wife's maid, Hagar, as his concubine. This was unquestionably against the will of God, who had already promised Abraham the following overwhelming blessings:

And I will make of thee a great nation, and I will bless thee, and make thy name great; and thou shalt be a blessing: And I will bless them that bless thee, and curse him that curseth thee: and in thee shall all families of the earth be blessed (Gen. 12:2,3).

Obviously, if God planned to make a great nation from Abraham, He would not have overlooked the detail of providing the patriarch a son and heir. As a matter of fact, He specifically promised the impatient Abraham a son by his own wife.

As we can well imagine, Hagar soon became unwilling to carry out her former role as a handmaiden. After all, she had given the master of the house a son. The situation soon became unbearable, and at length Hagar and Ishmael were banished.

But God did not forget Ishmael or write him off as the result of some unrighteous mistake. In the wilderness the Lord preserved Hagar and her son and made great promises to that side of the "family" as well:

And God heard the voice of the lad; and the angel of God called to Hagar out of heaven, and said unto her, What aileth thee, Hagar? fear not; for God hath heard the voice of the lad where he is. Arise, lift up the lad, and hold him in thine hand; for I will make him a great nation. And God opened her eyes, and she saw a well of water; and she went, and filled the bottle with water, and gave the lad drink (Gen. 21:17—19).

God gave His personal attention to the youth, Ishmael:

And God was with the lad; and he grew, and dwelt in

the wilderness, and became an archer. And he dwelt in the wilderness of Paran: and his mother took him a wife out of the land of Egypt (Gen. 21:20,21).

Thus we see that Ishmael, the seed of Abraham, was born of an Egyptian and married an Egyptian.

Meanwhile, Isaac had been born to Sarah in due course, according to God's promise. Ishmael was about fourteen years old when Isaac was born, and a sibling rivalry that we are still enduring today was begun.

God dealt more than fairly with the two heirs. At the time when He had promised that Isaac would be born, Abraham made a heartfelt plea on behalf of Ishmael:

And Abraham said unto God, O that Ishmael might live before thee! (Gen. 17:18).

God responded graciously, repeating His promise regarding Isaac:

And God said, Sarah thy wife shall bear thee a son indeed; and thou shalt call his name Isaac: and I will establish my covenant with him for an everlasting covenant, and with his seed after him (Gen. 17:19).

God still did not forget Ishmael:

And as for Ishmael, I have heard thee: Behold, I have blessed him, and will make him fruitful, and will multiply him exceedingly; twelve princes shall he beget, and I will make him a great nation (Gen. 17:20).

But He was emphatic about which of the two sons would have the valued covenant:

But my covenant will I establish with Isaac, which Sarah shall bear unto thee at this set time in the next year (Gen. 17:21).

Thus Ishmael married an Egyptian woman and became the father of the Arab nations. The Holy Book of Islam, the Koran, looks back to Abraham as the patriarch of that faith.

Isaac grew up to marry Rebecca, and to that couple were born the extraordinary twins, Jacob and Esau. If there had been rivalry between Isaac and Ishmael, there was real war between Jacob and Esau. They even struggled in their mother's womb, causing Rebecca to consult God about the antagonism within her. Jacob, whose name means "supplanter," was born actually grabbing his brother's heel! He was later to bear out the full meaning of his name when he cunningly persuaded Esau to give up his birthright.

What has all this to do with the history of Israel and Egypt? The twin brothers parted company at this time; each made a definitive and historic choice of wife. Jacob traveled to Haran and married Leah and then Rachel, daughters of his uncle Laban, out of Abraham's blood line. But Esau was not nearly so careful about his family heritage:

And Esau seeing that the daughters of Canaan pleased not Isaac his father; Then went Esau unto Ishmael, and took unto the wives which he had Mahalath the daughter of Ishmael Abraham's son, the sister of Nebajoth, to be his wife (Gen. 28:8,9).

Thus Esau, grandson to Abraham, born the heir to the covenant of God with the chosen people, became identified instead with the Egyptians. In a very real way, Esau is an ancestor of Anwar Sadat as Jacob is an ancestor of Begin. This first intermarriage between a covenanted Israelite and a woman of Egypt was the beginning of thousands of years of disagreement between these two nations. The first real reconciliation between the families of Egypt and Israel was not to take place until A.D. November 19, 1977!

Jacob and Esau themselves, however, did not remain mortal enemies for a lifetime. They were separated when Jacob went to Haran and Esau remained in the Holy Land. But some years later Jacob chose to return with his large family, servants, and animals. Jacob was deeply distressed when he learned that Esau would be coming to meet him with 400 men (Gen. 32:6)! Jacob prayed with humility:

And Jacob said, O God of my father Abraham, and God of my father Isaac, the LORD which saidst unto me, Return unto thy country, and to thy kindred, and I will deal well with thee: I am not worthy of the least of all the mercies, and of all the truth, which thou hast shewed unto thy servant; for with my staff I passed over this Jordan; and now I am become two bands. Deliver me, I pray thee, from the hand of my brother, from the hand of Esau: for I fear him, lest he will come and smite me, and the mother with the children. And thou saidst, I will surely do thee good, and make thy seed as the sand of the sea, which cannot be numbered for multitude (Gen. 32:9—12).

After reminding the Almighty of His divine promises, Jacob decided to prepare a gift for Esau to show his goodwill.

And he lodged there that same night; and took of that which came to his hand a present for Esau his brother; Two hundred she goats, and twenty he goats, two hundred ewes, and twenty rams, Thirty milch camels with their colts, forty kine, and ten bulls, twenty she asses, and ten foals (Gen. 32:13—15).

We cannot help but be reminded of the gifts Prime Minister Begin is willing to give the Egyptians at this time in order to achieve reconciliation and peace. Begin, the symbol of Jacob, the covenanted one, has good reason to be afraid of today's Egyptians, who have sworn to drive Israel into the sea. He is thus ready to placate the Egyptian ruler, within reason, as was his illustrious ancestor.

Jacob was at least as clever a negotiator as Begin. He did not order that all the gifts be delivered to Esau at once, but rather that the animals be spaced out, so that his brother would receive gift after gift. Jacob and his wives and children would remain at the rear; he hoped Esau would be greatly appeased by all that he had received.

And he delivered them into the hand of his servants,

every drove by themselves; and said unto his servants, Pass over before me, and put a space betwixt drove and drove. And he commanded the foremost, saying, When Esau my brother meeteth thee, and asketh thee, saying, Whose art thou? and whither goest thou? and whose are these before thee? Then thou shalt say, They be thy servant Jacob's; it is a present sent unto my lord Esau: and, behold, also he is behind us. And so commanded he the second, and the third, and all that followed the droves, saying, On this manner shall ye speak unto Esau, when ye find him. And say ye moreover, Behold, thy servant Jacob is behind us. For he said, I will appease him with the present that goeth before me, and afterward I will see his face; peradventure he will accept of me (Gen. 32:16—20).

Begin also offers a succession of concessions in exchange for peace. Goats, rams, and camels have become territory in the Sinai, self-government for the Palestinians, and so forth, as time has passed. But the style is recognizable and the result—real reconciliation—may be in the offing.

As Esau approached with his 400 men, he repeatedly received the lavish gifts presented him by Jacob's servants. Each servant did as he was bidden, announcing that his master awaited Esau in peace at the rear of their company.

Jacob's final ploy was to place his large family in the path of Esau, so that his brother could appreciate how good God had been to Jacob over the years.

And Jacob lifted up his eyes, and looked, and, behold, Esau came, and with him four hundred men. And he divided the children unto Leah, and unto Rachel, and unto the two handmaids. And he put the handmaids and their children foremost, and Leah and her children after, and Rachel and Joseph hindermost. And he passed over before them, and bowed himself to the ground seven times, until he came near to his brother. And Esau ran to meet him, and embraced him, and fell on his neck, and kissed him: and they wept. And he lifted up his eyes, and saw the women and the children; and said, Who are those with thee? And he said, The children which God hath graciously given thy servant (Gen. 33:1—5).

If we may stretch our analogy a little further, we are reminded of the galvanizing scene at Ben Gurion Airport as Anwar Sadat and Menachem Begin sincerely embraced. They very nearly wept, in the manner of Jacob and Esau, as the television cameras of the world looked on. Unquestionably, Anwar Sadat was warmly received as he descended from his Egyptian aircraft and crossed the red carpet, greeting one Israeli leader after another, as if to say, "Who are all these people?" The scene was almost identical to that electrifying reconciliation so long ago in the land of Canaan.

Perhaps even several of the ensuing developments in the Sadat-Begin negotiations are reflected in the remarkable story of the reconciliation of Jacob and Esau. President Sadat's recognition of Israel as a nation, a crucial ramification of his state visit, seems to be reflected by his ancestor: "And Esau said, I have enough, my brother; keep that thou hast unto thyself" (Gen. 33:9).

Are we actually seeing a modern version of the joyous reconciliation between Jacob and Esau?

Perhaps we are; the situation awaits further developments. But one thing is absolutely certain: We are experiencing the sovereignty of God.

The Hand of God

Looking once again at the overall developments in the startling new situation in the Middle East, we must surely see the hand of God working steadily in the affairs of men.

In one brief year, we saw a born-again Christian, vitally aware of biblical prophecy concerning Israel and the Middle East, elected president of the United States. We saw a most unlikely candidate rise to the high office of prime minister of Israel after the utterly unexpected fall of his illustrious predecessor. And the most extraordinary development of all—we saw the Pharaoh of modern Egypt undertake what he himself termed "a holy mission." Men working on their own and having the power to do anything they wish with the politics of the nations of the world could hardly have arrived at such a triumvirate of personalities devoted to immediate peace in the Middle East. Surely we are seeing the sovereignty of God.

We must appreciate, again, the startling brevity of time in which these events all took place as well as their remarkable cohesion. Although we couldn't have possibly predicted it even a matter of months ago, we stand now at the very hour of peace between Israel and Egypt, a situation which has not been achieved in 4,000 years!

God apparently continues to manage this complicated peace effort. After Sadat's departure from Israel, he became a marked man among his fair-weather friends of the various Arab nations. There were rumors of his imminent overthrow or even assassination. The Cairo Conference, which was to have followed the negotiations in Jerusalem, was poorly attended, to say the least. Only the United States, Egypt, and Israel finally sat down to try to advance the talks. The other Arab nations boycotted this further effort in a show of anger against the rebel from their ranks.

President Carter made every effort to assuage the enormous rivalries in the normally stormy League of Arab Nations. The leaders of Saudi Arabia, Jordan, and Syria were contacted in Carter's attempt to ease the way toward peace and to promote patience with the situation in Cairo.

It seems that the peace will be a reality. At the time of this writing, tempers have cooled and further negotiations have taken place. The road is a difficult one, full of treacherous curves, but it seems that somehow, in the sovereignty of God, peace will come. We can surely observe the progress, however painstaking, toward this worthy objective, and we can even more certainly depend upon the prophecies of divinely inspired Ezekiel.

There will be peace because the prophets saw it and wrote of it.

WORLD WAR III

But before there will be peace there will be war, according to the prophets.

The reader should carefully study Ezekiel 38 and 39:1—10, which give the details of the abortive Russian invasion of Israel. Because of the alliance of the many nations involved and the ferocity of this assault, it is fair to refer to this act of Satan as World War III.

The history of the young nation of Communist Russia records a predilection for violent expansion accompanied by the partial accomplishment of this deadly serious doctrine of world takeover. Russia as we know it today actually came into being in 1917, when the Bolshevik Revolution overthrew the czar. There was deep trouble in Russia for a while—first starvation and then an agonizingly slow recovery toward economic stability.

The internal unrest continued until the beginning of World War II, when Russia allied with the Axis powers in 1940. Declared war with Germany followed, and the world stood by in astonishment as the Russian war machine, inexperienced and in many respects archaic, finally outfought and overwhelmed the Nazis. By virtue of her pursuit of the armies of the Third Reich across Eastern Europe, Russia was able to occupy that territory, which she essentially never left. Eastern Europe was then under Communist domination.

Something called "peaceful coexistence" then prevailed, as communism from the Berlin Wall eastward, and capitalism in western Europe, pursued an uneasy accommodation. But in 1956 the bear began to show its claws. The nation of Hungary tried to revolt against the Communist overlords and was crushed by Moscow in a bloody and cruel police action. Tanks rumbled down the streets of Budapest as the citizenry cowered. In the same year Russia was drawn militarily into the Middle East over the Suez Canal event and the second of Israel's wars.

It was now clear that Russia had taken her place among the most powerful nations of the world economically, militarily, and scientifically. In the following year, when the first Russian Sputnik satellite was launched, the world had a new leader in space exploration as well.

Fearlessly Russia took on the United States in minor events, shooting down a U-2 spy plane in 1960 and attempting to deploy missiles in Cuba in 1962. Her obvious part in the Viet Nam war clearly displayed her animosity to the Americans. But in that period Russia also absorbed a humiliating defeat. In 1967 the Israelis overwhelmed Egypt, Syria, and Jordan—all armed to the teeth with the best of Russian military strategy and equipment—in just six days! Russia has never forgotten that devastating defeat.

Meanwhile, the Communists continued their iron-fisted hold over eastern Europe, crushing an uprising in Czechoslovakia in 1968. They gave their complete support to the North Vietnamese in 1969. In 1973, Russia again backed the Arabs—this time in greatest earnest—in the Yom Kippur War. For a time it did appear that Israel might see defeat in that terrifying sneak attack on the most holy day of the Jewish year. But once again the God of Israel and His armies prevailed. The Russians must have been totally astonished to see the Arabs and their sophisticated Kremlin weaponry fall back once again before the inexplicable might of the Jews.

Also in 1973, the concept of detente came into vogue, with the Soviet Union and the United States ostensibly pursuing policies of mutual accommodation. Nuclear war had to be avoided at any cost, of course, and the two superpowers struck up a "friendly" relationship. By 1975, Russia, by reason of its numerical strength, had become the world's most powerful nation militarily.

Since 1976, the Russian political situation has varied. There were serious troubles at home with agricultural failures, social unrest, and an uneasy relationship with Communist China. Border clashes with Russia's gigantic, powerful eastern neighbor began to increase, and disaffection among the vast population of the Soviet Union became common news. Alexander Solzhenitsyn's book, the *Gulag Archipelago*, revealed the horrors of Russian police and the terrorist methods used against their own population. For this reason, among others, the aging Kremlin leadership was being widely criticized internationally.

Most recently, Russia has demonstrated obvious expansionist policies on the continent of Africa, fostering insurrections and a Marxist philosophy in a number of the young nations there. At present, Communists cheer on the sidelines as such areas of unrest as Angola, Somalia, and South Africa tremble under the pressures of modern geopolitics.

As of this writing, the situation in outline is this: Russia wishes to expand into Africa, her next logical step after her European and Asian expansions, and the Middle East stands in her way— particularly Israel. Russia has been able to accommodate the Arabs in the past and make alliances by means of weapons agreements and military advice. But Russia has never been able to cultivate the Israelis and has never really tried. Israel and Russia stand in total opposition when matters of politics and spiritual issues are involved.

God Versus Russia

It is clear from Ezekiel 38 and 39 that the battle we are calling World War III is between God and Russia. If the Russians think they are taking on only Israel when they attempt to invade that special land, they are disastrously unaware of history.

The Bible records the destruction of great empires who sought to invade Israel and destroy the chosen people of God. The Babylonians, the Persians, Alexander's Greeks, and the Roman Empire comprise a list of ancient civilizations destroyed because of their animosity to God's people. By contrast, the Jews, weak in numbers but tireless in spirit, again occupy the land God gave to their fathers.

At this time Russia is about to take her place among those unfortunate nations who thought they had found the "final solution" to the "Jewish problem."

Ezekiel clearly sets down the instructions of God concerning this dramatic prophecy. Examining chapter 38, we can see in verse 2 that Ezekiel has been told to set his face against Gog, the land of Magog, and the chief prince of Meshech and Tubal. Many genealogical studies—such as Hal Lindsey's *The Late Great Planet Earth* and *The Coming Russian Invasion of Israel*, by Thomas S. McCall and Zola Levitt—demonstrate that the territories of Gog and Magog and the provinces of Meshech and Tubal (Moscow and Tobolsk) are now encompassed by Russia. They also point out that Genesis 10 reveals the names of Noah's grandsons, in which list are found all the names in Ezekiel 38—Gomer, Magog, Meshech, Tubal, Togarmah, and so on.

Here suffice it to say that the geographical area involved encompasses eastern Europe and northern Asia, lands adjacent to the Middle East. These territories were originally settled by founders whose names were kept through the generations in the same manner that we named our cities and states in this nation after their founders (Pennsylvania, Pittsburgh, Williamsport). If we give the territories described in the prophecy their present-day names, we recognize a tactical encirclement of Israel for the purposes of this invasion.

In verse 4 we read that God will put hooks in the jaws of the invaders to turn them back. The Almighty's position on this invasion is explicit. He says in verse 3, "I am against thee." The God of Israel will not allow His Holy Land, restored to its rightful owners, to be destroyed by this massive assault. He intends to take a hand in the battle, and when God says, "I am against you," the battle is over. The shields, helmets, bows and arrows described by Ezekiel should be thought of as their modern counterparts—missiles, tanks, and aircraft. The prophecy says Russia shall "ascend and be like a storm, and come like a cloud to cover the land." The reference certainly seems to be to airborne forces, with which Russia is very well-equipped.

Ezekiel 38:5 begins to detail the satellite nations of Russia who will comprise the allies in the invasion. In Ezekiel's time, Persia was made up of parts of modern Iraq, Iran, and Turkey. One can easily foresee these modern nations cooperating with Russia in a war against Israel. Ancient Ethiopia, which of course still exists today, in Ezekiel's time covered a large part of the continent of Africa to the south of Egypt. Today, now that the monarchy of King Haile Selassie has fallen and been replaced by an unsteady military regime, this formerly pro-western nation has turned toward an alliance with Russia. The great progress made by Communism in Africa in the past few years will become increasingly evident as Ethiopia takes her place in the coming invasion. Libya, which existed in Ezekiel's time as a reliable enemy of Israel, certainly still plays that role. The Libyans today, under their fanatical military dictatorship, are passionately anti-Israel. They will welcome a chance to express their hostility under a protective alliance with powerful Russia.

Gomer, which we mentioned above, is the land of the descendants of Noah who migrated toward eastern Europe. Gomer today encompasses the area we know as East Germany, Poland, and the other east European countries that lie behind the iron curtain. It is fascinating to consider that Germany may have been divided by the will of God after World War II. The descendants of Gomer live in what we now regard as East Germany, and it will be those people who participate with Russia in this invasion. By authority of the Word of God, the nation of Germany will not be reunited before the coming war.

Ezekiel also mentions the province of Togarmah, which lies south of Moscow, or Meshech, and covers much of the highly industrialized area of the eastern part of Russia. Togarmah will be vital to the invasion as the supplier of the enormous amount of weaponry needed by all these allied forces. We have already experienced the might of Russia in the form of large amounts of war materials sent to foreign nations. Togarmah has always produced a certain basic military vehicle—the horse, or the modern tank. At one time the Russian Cossacks who lived in the province of Togarmah were considered the finest military horsemen in the world. Today they produce some of the world's finest tanks. Their talents along these lines will figure seriously in World War III.

Communism and War

Russia today represents two phenomena. First is her overriding political ideology, which we know as communism. And second, stemming from the communist ideal, is Russia's military machine. The philosophy of communism and the escalation of

Russian military control have tended to burgeon at different rates throughout the world. For example, in eastern Europe Russia dominates the satellite nations militarily. But there remains in those nations an uneasiness about Kremlin-style Communism. Such issues as basic human rights continue to surface in the territories Russia has overtaken by force, and the Communists are obliged to enter into such agreements as the Helsinki Pact. Russia may conquer geographical territories relatively easily, but she cannot always rule the minds of the population.

Thus God says through Ezekiel two seemingly opposite things: "I will turn thee back" and "I will bring thee forth." Recent history clearly shows Russia advancing by fits and starts, seemingly very much under control of Almighty God.

Prior to 1956, Russia was only minimally involved in the Middle East. But in that year Egypt, under the leadership of Nasser, seized control of the Suez Canal from England and France. Those two nations immediately armed to retake the canal. Then Russia took a position. She immediately offered aid to Egypt and announced to England and France that they should take no action in the Middle East. Russia was heavily armed too, of course. The United States was forced into asking England and France to refrain from military action over the canal incident in order to keep peace.

This was Russia's initial commitment to the Middle East. She would stand by Egypt and the other Arab nations, she said, against any aggressors. Hooks had been put into her jaws, in the words of Ezekiel, and now she had been drawn into God's central arena of operations—the Middle East.

It was Israel—not England and France—who moved militarily against Egypt. Through Israel's action England and France were able to secure the Suez Canal. The Israelis had important reasons for their reaction, reasons that go back to the year 1917, during World War I. In order to understand the positions involved in the Middle East at the time Russia entered the conflict, we must retrace the steps by which Israel became a power to be reckoned with.

In 1917, British General Allenby led an allied force into the Holy Land against the occupying Turks. Miraculously, Allenby was able to capture the Holy Land, and he took the city of Jerusalem without firing a shot! The Turks fled their entrenchments there with no resistance. It seems that the name of Allenby had struck fear in their hearts, for it means "a man sent from God."

Thus Britain began serving as the protector of what was then called Palestine—actually the biblical land of Israel.

The British occupation of Palestine presented a favorable opportunity for Zionist Jews who wished to return to the land of Israel. Certainly the British were more amenable than the Turks to discussing such a return. Conferences were held before the British Parliament, with Jewish leaders asking for permission for the Jews to reoccupy their promised land. Out of those conferences came the Balfour Agreement, which set aside an area in Palestine for those Jews who wished to return.

It should be appreciated, however, that the majority of the world's Jewish population did not really prefer to return. They had established themselves, particularly in Europe, and had become influential. They were not the most popular people in any nation, often having to live behind barred windows and locked gates, yet they were among the masters in Europe. Some of them had come to control great wealth and were eminently successful in the lively commerce of twentieth-century Europe.

Thus, similar to the majority of Jews in the dispersion to Babylon in the sixth century before Christ, many were loathe to return to the wilderness of Israel. True, the land had once flowed with milk and honey and had been very fruitful. But throughout the long centuries of Arab and Turkish occupation, it had become a desert, declared by some to be almost uninhabitable. Only a remnant chose to return at this time. One is reminded of the days of Nehemiah, when the city of Jerusalem was slowly rebuilt by a faithful few.

For these reasons the Israelis more or less owed a favor to Great Britain in 1956. The English Parliament had, after all, allowed the first return of the Jews to Palestine in nineteen centuries! When the canal issue became heated, the British called upon Israeli Prime Minister David Ben Gurion, who had originally approached Parliament and helped effect the Balfour Agreement. The British asked Ben Gurion to use Israel's military power against Egypt to seize the Suez Canal. Israel agreed.

Israel had been invariably successful against her Arab neighbors, and particularly against Egypt. She had won her war of independence in 1947 and had been declared a nation in 1948. In the years until 1956 there had been several armed clashes along the borders, but Israel had held her own. Now she was ready to try her military strength against Egypt.

The Israelis proved to be more than equal to the occasion. They moved through the Gaza Strip and the Sinai Peninsula, pushing the Egyptian forces back to the Suez Canal. When the fighting was at its most intense, Britain and France came forth with an ultimatum. They declared that if both Israel and Egypt persisted in battle for twelve hours, Britain and France would attack them both for the "protection" of the canal.

Naturally, Britain and France had engineered the entire situation. They merely wanted to end up where they started—in control of the canal. The twelve-hour period expired and the fighting continued. That gave the British and French navies, paratroopers, and aircraft their excuse. As they threw themselves into the fight, the world observed a curious phenomenon. All the shells, bombs, and attacks by the paratroops seemed to fall on the Egyptians. Not a single Israeli was even wounded by the European attack. Obviously, the entire altercation had been orchestrated to perpetrate European control of the canal and to punish the Egyptians for seizing it.

But what about Russia's threat of intervention? Indeed, Russia immediately mobilized to make good on her warning, and military forces were assembled to attack the Middle East. The action that had been taken by Britain and France had "hooked" the Russian military and drawn them toward God's theater of operations.

However, Russia was suddenly distracted from coming to Egypt's aid by an uprising in Europe. At just that time a group of freedom fighters in Hungary rose up and started to battle the Russian occupational forces. In order to put down this rebellion, Russia was obliged to divert twelve divisions of tanks to Hungary. The cruel slaughter in Budapest, when the Communists gave new meaning to the term "overkill," is well remembered by the whole world.

Communism was once again in control in Hungary after the revolt was subdued, but it lost face in many areas of the world and has not since regained its influence. In truth, the brutal Hungarian massacre was seemingly used by God to hinder the rapid advance of communism and to strike what would eventually become a death blow to that ideology.

So it is clear that God allowed two unique events. He "turned back" the political ideology of communism, and He "brought forth" the Russian military machine into the Middle East. Eventually, of course, communism will fall under the newer and even more totalitarian regime of the Antichrist. And Russian military might will be utterly eliminated in the future invasion of the Middle East.

In the Latter Days

Now, recognizing the major outlines behind this upcoming invasion of the Middle East by Russia, we can return for the details to the pronouncements of the prophet Ezekiel. In 38:8 the prophet indicates that this invasion will come "in the latter years." The prophet goes on in the same verse to describe an Israel which is "brought back from the sword and is gathered out of many people." This very clearly describes modern Israel (and remember that it was originally spoken during another dispersion some twenty-five centuries ago!). Israel was certainly brought back from the sword, created directly out of the destruction of World War II; and its population is certainly gathered out of many nations.

The prophet also describes the invasion as being against a people who are enjoying a period of peace. The invader will say, "I will go up to the land of unwalled villages; I will go to them that are at rest, dwelling safely with windows having neither bars nor gates. ..." This time of safety, according to Verses 11 and 14, will be the time when the Russians invade. Verse 13 seems to suggest that Israel has committed allies, and they too recognize Russia's desire to conquer Israel and control the Middle East. These are named Sheba and Dedan, who represent the few Arab and Mediterranean nations sympathetic toward Israel's situation.

The major allies of Israel are identified by recognizing the modern counterparts of the "merchants of Tarshish, with all the young lions thereof," in Ezekiel's terminology. The ancient city of Tarshish on the Mediterranean Sea once did a vigorous merchant business, trading goods with the seafaring nations that would one day become the Roman Empire. Those nations faded away, of course, with the later collapse of the Roman Empire, but the territorial divisions still remain just as with the allies of Russia.

Out of the merchants of Tarshish came the colonial empires, of which the most successful was Great Britain. At one time Great Britain controlled an empire upon which the sun never set. And its symbol, the lion, reigned around the world. No other empire had more "young lions" than did Great Britain. Presently the young lions are Canada, Australia, New Zealand, South Africa, and the United States. The old lion has become weak and takes his place in the pack. And the mightiest of the young lions, the United States, is now the leader. So, conceivably, we find among the allies of Israel the nations of Western Europe, plus the young lions of the New World under the leadership of the United States.

Something very similar to this situation is occurring on the world scene today. Russia indeed is making rumblings about the Middle East and is finding it most uncomfortable to see peace established in that area. The free nations of Western Europe and the United States stand in opposition to Russia's Middle East policies. Ezekiel's prophetic vision can be interpreted even more explicitly as world events progress. The United States, in fact, is bound by an agreement made after the Suez event in 1956 to defend Israel. Israel obtained a protection agreement from the United States in return for withdrawing her forces from the canal area and giving the territory back to Egypt. President Dwight Eisenhower and Prime Minister David Ben Gurion came to an agreement at that time through the Israeli ambassador to Washington, Mrs. Golda Meir. The Gaza Strip and Sinai territories were returned to Egypt in consideration of an alliance between Israel and the United States, with the latter promising to defend Israel in time of need. Indeed twice since the agreement—in 1967 and 1973—the Americans have moved naval and military equipment rapidly to the aid of Israel.

In 1967 the Israelis took back Jerusalem, their first possession of that city in over 2500 years. Israelis had lived in the city in the second temple times, but always under the dictation of a foreign power. But now the prophecy of Jesus Christ in Luke 21:24 is reaching fulfillment: "Jerusalem shall be trodden down of the Gentiles, until the times of the Gentiles be fulfilled."

With the recovery of Jerusalem, another important piece of the prophetic puzzle fell into place. The Church Age is now apparently at its close. We must begin to look eagerly toward the appearance of Jesus Christ, for in that same chapter of Luke, Jesus said that when we see these things come to pass, we are to look up, for our redemption is "drawing nigh."

The defeat of the Arabs by Israel in 1967, and again in 1973, has placed Russia at a great disadvantage in the Middle East. She has lost her ability to maintain influence by diplomacy. It seems the only avenue left to her in that part of the world is military conquest. The best of Russian strategy and military hardware has still not seen success against Israel and God. Russia will seek revenge!

The peacetime during which Russia will take that action against Israel is beginning to flourish. The first step has been taken, as pointed out above, by Egypt and Israel. When there is an era of peace in Israel, Russia will strike!

God Versus Gog

The God of Israel will become truly angry at Russia's plan:

And it shall come to pass at the same time when Gog shall come against the land of Israel, saith the Lord GOD, that my fury shall come up in my face (Ezek. 38:18).

Reading through the rest of Ezekiel 38, we discover that Russia will move down from the north with her vast military machine and her allies, but in the mountains north of Israel the invasion will be stopped. In verse 21, God says He will call for a sword against Russia. An earthquake is also spoken of, as well as overflowing rain with much hail, pestilence, and blood.

If we are to take these passages as written, nature itself will oppose the Russians. The huge rain full of hail will hinder the movements of heavy mechanized equipment and stop the aircraft and their electronic gear. God also speaks of fire and brimstone falling on the vast army. Divine intervention in this battle is very apparent. In 39:3 God declares a plague on the invaders. There will be utter loss! Only one-sixth of the Russian population will escape this overwhelming destruction.

Some have said that Israel and her allies will use their nuclear warheads against Russia. The Scriptures do seem to indicate an intensity of warfare that justifies this interpretation. The war is over, it seems, in a moment.

God gives His reasons at the end of chapter 39 for this stunning conquest of Russia. Israel will recognize the hand of God and the Scriptures will be exalted. The heathen nations will realize that Israel, with God, is invincible. The Russian invasion of Israel is truly a story of a major earthly power trying to take on the God of creation.

The results are quite predictable.

"The War to End All Wars"

We should realize that the Russian invasion of Israel is *not* the war to end all wars. That distinction is reserved for the fearful Armageddon.

The Russian invasion is fought in the mountains of Israel north of Jerusalem, between Russia and her satellites and Israel and her allies. The victor is Israel. Ezekiel specifies that it will take Israel seven years to burn up the weapons Russia brings to the field of battle. This seven-year period is extremely significant in that it is the same amount of time given to the Tribulation period in Scripture. If the Russian invasion were part of Armageddon, then this seven-year burning of the weapons (as well as the seven-month burial of the dead, also stressed by Ezekiel) would extend into the Kingdom period. It is hard to picture such macabre events taking place while the King is on His throne in Jerusalem and peace reigns on the earth. Rather, it is more logical to assume that the Russian invasion of Israel comes at the outset of the Tribulation period, and that Israel cleanses the land just in time for the arrival of her King.

Armageddon occurs in the final moments of the Tribulation period. It is fought on the plains of Megiddo in the north of Israel between the Antichrist and his armies and the Lord Jesus Christ and His heavenly hosts.

Just before the time of World War III—the Russian invasion of Israel—the Lord Jesus Christ will descend from heaven with a shout and take His church out of the world (1 Thess. 4:16,17). This will remove any hindrance to the revealing of the man who is to become the Antichrist (2 Thess. 2:6—9). Therefore, as the time of the Russian invasion of Israel draws nearer, we find ourselves on the threshold of the appearance of Jesus Christ. It is not so important that we as believers realize the fine details of the upcoming battle; rather, we must recognize these sure signs of the imminent coming of our Lord.

The signs are evident all around us. Already that era of peace is being set up in the Middle East. Russia harbors a great animosity toward Israel, while the alliance of the United States and the free world nations supports Israel. The allies of the invader continue to fall into their prophesied roles. We have not even included the many signs of the end announced by the Lord Himself, such as famine, pestilence, earthquakes, and the like.

It is time to think in terms of destinies. If we pray for the Russian people, some of them will escape the destiny announced for them. If we pray for Egypt and review carefully the prophecies about that ancient nation, God will hear our prayers and spare some of the Egyptians. And if we, with the psalmist, "pray for the peace of Jerusalem," we will be appealing to God to lighten the horrible burdens that will be placed on His chosen people in the Tribulation period to come.

We certainly can do nothing to change the course of Russia or the facts of the Russian invasion—"It is written." But we can do everything possible to prepare ourselves and as many of our fellow men as we can for what lies ahead in God's plan. One thousand years of peace, and then eternity, lie beyond the devastation to come. Let us look toward that time in hope and prayer, while God does what He must about the situations here on a devastated earth.

4

"I AM AGAINST THEE, O GOG!"

As we said at the beginning of this book, the peace that will soon be achieved in the Middle East will serve only as a signal for a vicious war. The astute apostle Paul is our source, as he explained that "sudden destruction" would come among those who felt secure in "peace and safety" (1 Thess. 5:3).

As we read Ezekiel 38 and 39, the ferocity of the Russian invasion of Israel is stunning. Magog (the biblical name) will fall upon the Holy Land in a surprise attack in a time of peace. Her leader, Gog, will seek to "take a spoil." Gog apparently will believe that Israel is unprepared for a sudden invasion, an assumption which may be correct.

But his plans will be a total disaster. God is perfectly ready for such an invasion; He ominously declared through the prophet Ezekiel, "Behold, I am against thee, O Gog!" (Ezek. 38:3). Apparently , in a single day God will destroy the Russian army and five-sixths of the Russian population (Ezek. 38:4; 39:2). The two chapters of Ezekiel 38 and 39 express the righteous might of Jehovah and His utter wrath against those who would presume to invade the Promised Land.

God will be working directly with His chosen people again. God has been dealing indirectly with Israel for a long time, leading her to the very point of the Tribulation period. The magnificent prophecy of the Seventy Weeks of Years of the prophet Daniel (Dan. 9:24—27) makes clear that Israel and the world have a destiny yet to be accomplished in God's plan. The first sixty-nine of Daniel's weeks have been fulfilled; they led to the coming of the Messiah (v. 25: each of Daniel's weeks represents seven years. The Messiah came to Israel some 483 years after the starting point of the prophecy). There are seven years yet to come in this remarkable calendar of the future given by the angel to Daniel.

God has paused between His sixty-ninth and seventieth week to call out the church, the Body of Christ. He still deals with His chosen people—a remnant of Jews is saved in each generation—but God is calling *the entire world* to repentance and salvation (Acts 11:18). The church has existed for more than nineteen centuries, but she is being particularly energized in these last days, which suggests the imminent approach of those last seven years, commonly referred to as "the Tribulation period."

The Sword of the Lord

God will vanquish Russia and her allies in the coming invasion, and that act will represent a new era of the direct dealings of God with Israel. God's intervention on Israel's behalf will be reminiscent of those magnificent divine interventions found throughout the long story of invasions and battles of the Old Testament. God will direct Israel again, guaranteeing their borders, protecting them against pagans, and causing a new spirit of worship to fall upon the Holy Land.

Often in the Old Testament, powerful enemies fell upon Israel—enemies capable of utterly annihilating the chosen people. But God intervened. Marvelous miracles occurred in the times of Joshua, Gideon, David, the kings, and on and on as Jehovah preserved His people and subdued all invaders. The consequences of invading Israel have always been drastic. Mighty civilizations have come and gone while the Jews have been restored to their land.

God stopped Pharaoh and his army of chariots as the Hebrew people fled across the Red Sea. God inspired the faithful Samson to destroy a thousand Philistines with the jawbone of an ass. Gideon had only 300 men and faith in the God of Israel as he faced more than 100,000 encamped Midianites, but "the sword of the Lord and of Gideon" prevailed.

We could certainly continue to list example after example of the divine protection of Israel.

We now stand on the verge of another of those miraculous divine protections of the Holy Land. God will smash Russia as He smashed the entire Roman Empire, Alexander the Great, mighty ancient Persia, and the hosts of Babylon. It will be no contest, and someday in the future it will be as difficult to find Russia's remains as it now is to uncover the relics of those formerly mighty, but now extinct, empires.

We might say a word about the Christian church in Russia (and by the "Christian church" we mean the Spirit-led, born-again people). It is the eyewitness testimony of many visitors to Russia that the worship of the Lord Jesus is progressing in that nation, and that while the numbers are few, the believers are strong. The Communist government has not been able to keep God out of Russia nor prevent the Holy Spirit from working in the hearts of the Russian people. God has surely not forgotten this enormous population of human hearts which labor under an atheistic oppression.

Jesus instructed us:

Watch ye therefore, and pray always, that ye may be accounted worthy to escape all these things that shall come to pass, and to stand before the Son of man (Luke 21:36).

Here the Lord referred to things that "shall come to pass," rather than present things. Those words of our Lord do not exclude any people—not the

Americans, not the Egyptians or Israelis, and most certainly not the Russians.

The Russian invasion of Israel, described so completely in Ezekiel 38 and 39, is also covered by the apostle John in Revelation 6.

John begins in chapter 5 with the description of a book sealed with seven seals. At first there seem to be none worthy of opening this book, but then:

And one of the elders saith unto me, Weep not: behold, the Lion of the tribe of Juda, the Root of David, hath prevailed to open the book, and to loose the seven seals thereof (Rev. 5:5).

In Revelation 5, the Lord takes the book from His Father's hand. In Revelation 6, He opens the book and the first seal reveals a man on a white horse. This man "went forth conquering, and to conquer" (Rev. 6:2). This man is none other than the Antichrist.

And where is the church when the Antichrist is revealed to do his evil work? The church, comprised of those who were ready to escape from the "things that shall be," is in heaven.

Paul also indicated that the church would be taken to heaven before the Antichrist would be revealed:

Let no man deceive you by any means: for that day shall not come, except there come a falling away first, and that man of sin be revealed, the son of perdition; Who opposeth and exalteth himself above all that is called God, or that is worshipped; so that he as God sitteth in the temple of God, shewing himself that he is

God. Remember ye not, that, when I was yet with you, I told you these things? And now ye know what withholdeth that he might be revealed in his time. For the mystery of iniquity doth already work: only he who now letteth will let, until he be taken out of the way. And then shall that Wicked be revealed, whom the Lord shall consume with the spirit of His mouth, and shall destroy with the brightness of His coming (2 Thess. 2:3—8).

To paraphrase those final verses: There is certainly iniquity in the world now, but the Holy Spirit holds back evil. The Holy Spirit lives in the church; when the church departs, then the wicked one—the son of perdition, the man of sin, the one who imitates God—will be revealed.

The question of the Rapture of the church and its relationship to the Tribulation period meets with much discussion these days. Most passages in the Bible support the theory of a pre-Tribulation Rapture. If this is true, the church is to be taken out of the world before the Antichrist is revealed and the Tribulation period gets underway. This is an important fact for all Christians to reckon with, and a matter of life and death for the Russian believers. While Russia will be vanquished by the Lord, her true believers will be safe in heaven, near the Father's throne.

The second seal (Rev. 6:3,4) reveals a red horse whose rider, with enormous power, will take peace from the earth. We might consider these important verses in full:

And when he had opened the second seal, I heard the second beast say, Come and see. And there went out another horse that was red: and power was given to him that sat thereon to take peace from the earth, and that they should kill one another: and there was given unto him a great sword.

It is most interesting that the red horse represents the first act of war in the Tribulation period. The other prophecy, as we have seen, identifies the attack of the Red army against Israel as the beginning of that period. Clearly, Russian Christians, along with all the other believers of the world, will be standing before the throne of the Father at the time the terrible red horse is let loose upon the remainder of the earth's population.

God has not forgotten any detail and He certainly has not forgotten any believer.

The Destiny of Egypt

Egypt does not take part in the Russian invasion of Israel, according to the prophet Ezekiel.

Ezekiel's list of Magog's allies include Persia, Ethiopia, Libya, Gomer (Eastern Europe), and Togarmah (the Cossack country in southern Russia) (Ezek. 38:5,6). Egypt is not among those allies.

A glance at a world map will demonstrate that the allies' territory encircles Israel, creating a powerful invasion force indeed. Some might say that the prophet could have been making reasonable guesses as to the future enemies of Israel when he cited Persia, Libya, and Ethiopia, but only God could have known that Magog (Gen. 10:2) would someday conquer all of Eastern Europe and the southern territories next to the Middle East.

Indeed, by this geography lesson alone one can place the time of Ezekiel's long-range forecast. A century ago, for example, Russia would not have controlled those particular territories.

But where is Egypt, Israel's perennial enemy? Geographically, she certainly would have a place in this encircling assault, and indeed would be the closest to Israel of all those nations cited in this invasion. Could today's peace treaties between Egypt and Israel neutralize the country of Egypt so that, bound by a peace covenant in the future, she cannot rightfully attack her neighbor?

Whatever the case, Egypt's destiny is different. Ezekiel only mentions this land in passing as he talks about the Russian invasion. But the prophet Isaiah devoted an entire chapter to what he termed "the burden of Egypt." In this singularly illuminating and complex chapter, Isaiah 19, we may find secrets of the ages which only can be clarified by today's events.

In all prophecy there are subtleties and nuances difficult for modern readers to fathom. The prophecies of Isaiah 19, for example, have been interpreted different ways by different scholars. Certainly, however, the passage of time makes biblical predictions easier. A good example would be the "dry bones" vision of Ezekiel, mentioned earlier. Prophecy scholars through the ages were puzzled as to the literal meaning of the Jewish homecoming. After all, it became very difficult to believe that this scattered, persecuted people would live to reoccupy their Promised Land.

Many confusions arose—even false doctrine and whole systems of erroneous theology—because the prophecy seemed so unlikely. But after 1948, those who questioned the literal rendition of the prophecy were silenced. Israel was restored just as the prophet said, and one more complex prophecy was fully understood.

We are in a similar dilemma when we try to deal with Isaiah 19 and Egypt. Some of the chapter has not been fulfilled as yet, and some of it can reasonably be construed to apply to Egypt's past behavior. But in any case, today's startling events in Egypt seem to correlate so well with Isaiah's verses that the chapter resembles a modern newscast.

Isaiah begins this way:

The burden of Egypt. Behold, the LORD rideth upon a swift cloud, and shall come into Egypt: and the idols of Egypt shall be moved at His presence, and the heart of Egypt shall melt in the midst of it. And I will set the Egyptians against the Egyptians: and they shall fight every one against his brother, and every one against his neighbor; city against city, and kingdom against kingdom (Isa. 19:1,2).

Some of these drastic prophecies are in the process of developing today in Egypt. Despite the recent maneuvering for peace across the border, Egypt is not a nation at peace with itself. Egypt is now, and has been before in modern times, an oppressor of Israel; we fully realize that God deals with those who rise against the Jews.

Isaiah seems to tell us that the spirit of Egypt—

the morale and self-confidence of its people—is going to be so shaken that that nation will be thrown into a state of real unrest. Perhaps Egypt pursuing peace with Israel is a sign of God's beginning to undermine the Egyptian confidence and spirit. Indeed it would not be a biblical precedent for Israel to be used by God to trouble the Egyptians.

It is no secret that Egypt is fearful of Israel's military might and firepower. The Egyptian man on the street realizes he faces a nuclear power in Israel, while Egypt, at present, is relatively weak. Isaiah's statement that God will set the Egyptians against the Egyptians seems to describe a revolution or civil war within that nation. Any nation that suffers the loss of personal security and self assurance suffers an atmosphere conducive to civil war. Americans returning from Egypt testify concerning the economic chaos and social instability of that land.

According to Isaiah, the Egyptians will seek a solution they have utilized in the past:

And the spirit of Egypt shall fail in the midst thereof; and I will destroy the counsel thereof: and they shall seek to the idols, and to the charmers, and to them that have familiar spirits, and to the wizards (Isa. 19:3).

In ancient days, Pharaoh turned in times of trouble to his magicians, the idols of Egypt, and the "familiar spirits and wizards" that the Egyptians believed would give them good counsel. Egypt is the chief symbol of idolatry in much of the Old Testament; God even forbade the people of Judah to retreat to that pagan land in the face of Nebuchadnezzar's invasion. (When they did retreat, God prophesied against them severely and none of them survived.) Modern Egypt will apparently seek solutions to its various dilemmas in the ancient realm of demonic powers. Scripture, of course, forbids such involvement, and we gather that Egypt will be brought to total collapse for seeking such counsel.

Of course, Americans indulge in the same heresy. In this country we have no dearth of clairvoyants, sorcerers, astrologists, mediums, and the like. Witchcraft flourishes here and the signs of the zodiac are printed in the newspapers every day. Many people schedule their lives according to these "familiar spirits and wizards," in defiance of biblical prohibitions. Perhaps we could apply the wisdom of Isaiah to our own situation; we are experiencing a time of turmoil in this nation, and like Egypt, some of our people are turning to heathen practices as a result.

The ancient pagan counsel of Egypt will utterly fail that country. Isaiah goes on to say:

And the Egyptians will I give over into the hand of a cruel lord; and a fierce king shall rule over them, saith the Lord, the LORD of hosts (Isa. 19:4).

Some people thought former President Gamel Abdul Nasser was this "cruel lord" of whom Isaiah spoke. The upheaval in Egypt was tremendous at the time Nasser came to power, deposing King

Farouk. But even at the height of the clamor over Nasser's rise, Egypt was not in civil war.

President Sadat is also considered a cruel lord in some ways. His ascension was marked by purges of the government, by prison sentences and executions, and by serious unrest in the land. Sadat is undoubtedly a very cunning and crafty ruler whose mild outward appearance is belied by his ability to move swiftly to maintain his authority. But as time has passed, and especially as we have seen President Sadat make what seems to be the most genuine of peace offerings toward Israel, we must look to the future for this cruel lord spoken of by Isaiah.

Of course, the Antichrist himself would adequately fit Isaiah's description. This ruler, who will come during the Tribulation period, will apparently deal as harshly with Egypt as he will with Israel.

Isaiah goes on to describe still more burdens for Egypt:

And the waters shall fail from the sea, and the river shall be wasted and dried up. And they shall turn the rivers far away; and the brooks of defence shall be emptied and dried up: the reeds and flags shall wither (Isa. 19:5,6).

Isaiah indicates that the system of rivers in Egypt is to be seriously affected by some series of events. We are in an excellent position to appreciate this particular prophecy because of the relatively recent construction of the Aswan Dam, which regulates the flow of the Nile River. The dam was constructed by Nasser and dedicated by president-elect Sadat a few years ago. Nasser had every hope that the dam would produce some much-needed economic wealth for his nation, but it has turned out to be a very mixed blessing. The money and engineers for the construction of this massive dam were provided by Russia, after the United States refused to participate.

As it happened though, it's just as well that our nation had little to do with the dam, for it has precipitated an ecological disaster.

The dam has produced an adverse effect upon agriculture, industries, and the natural balance of the territory along the banks of the Nile River. The fishing, the textile, and paper industries—all located along the Nile and its branches—have been vastly curtailed. Note the ancient prophet's rendition of this point:

The paper reeds by the brooks, by the mouth of the brooks, and every thing sown by the brooks, shall wither, be driven away, and be no more. The fishers also shall mourn, and all they that cast angle into the brooks shall lament, and they that spread nets upon the waters shall languish. Moreover they that work in fine flax, and they that weave networks, shall be confounded. And they shall be broken in the purposes thereof, all that make sluices and ponds for fish (Isa. 19:7—10).

A scientific analysis given by Dr. Leonard Riffale in the *Dallas Morning News* dealt with the problem:

Before the Aswan Dam became operational in 1954, the United Arab Republic's (Egypt's) annual Mediterranean catch of fish averaged about 106 thousand metric tons. The figures have dropped now to a low of 85 thousand tons. The sardine catch, which has been averaging 15 thousand tons a year, by 1966, just two years after the dam went into operation, dropped to 544 tons.

Obviously, this part of the Egyptian fishing industry has been virtually wiped out by the presence of the dam. Dr. Riffale goes on:

It seems that the dam has cut off the flow of phosphates and nitrates and other nutrients on which fish along the coast were thriving. This drop in the water's fertility has discouraged concentration of fish in that area and has nearly halted concentration of fish in that region. The troubles caused by the Aswan Dam don't stop with the fish. The dam prevents the Nile from depositing silt that it formerly piled up along the coast. Furthermore, there seems to be no way to control an ever-increasing saltiness of coastal waters. Eventually, this will happen to the area's lake water also. All in all, it seems the Aswan Dam is making quite a mess out of the Nile River, which at one time was apparently a very delicately balanced ecological region.

Not only were the fishing and other industries along the Nile banks affected, but Egypt nearly lost the colossal sculptures of Abu Simbel, which have stood for thirty-two centuries. These four massive statues of Pharoah Ramses II are carved out of a mountain at what used to be a site well above the Nile River. But as the water rose behind the Aswan Dam, the monumental statuary was threatened by the river waters. Finally, money for a conservation project was allotted by UNESCO, an agency of the United Nations. The statues were carved into massive blocks and reassembled 200 feet above the original site. They are now safe from the rising waters.

Let us again hear that strange echo from the prophet Isaiah: "Behold ... the idols of Egypt shall be moved ..." (Isa. 19:1).

In his next three verses, Isaiah refers to the fact that wisdom is lacking in Egypt and Pharaoh has no reliable advisor to whom he can turn in times of great trouble. The Almighty is almost sarcastic as He speaks through the great prophet to the modern Pharoah:

Surely the princes of Zoan are fools, the counsel of the wise counsellors of Pharaoh is become brutish: how say ye unto Pharaoh, I am the son of the wise, the son of ancient kings? Where are they? where are thy wise men? And let them tell thee now, and let them know what the LORD of hosts hath purposed upon Egypt. The princes of Zoan are become fools, the princes of Noph are deceived; they have also seduced Egypt, even they that are the stay of the tribes thereof (Isa. 19:11—13).

President Sadat has few technologically educated experts to combat the difficult problems confronting modern Egypt. The Russians, of course, advised Sadat for a time, but the Russians helped create this entire problem in the first place. In any case, they are long gone and, as Ezekiel pointed out, no ally of Egypt anymore.

Now Isaiah stresses problems of increasing gravity. The very heart of Egypt is affected and the people are weak:

The LORD hath mingled a perverse spirit in the midst thereof: and they have caused Egypt to err in every work thereof, as a drunken man staggereth in his vomit. Neither shall there be any work for Egypt, which the head or tail, branch or rush, may do. In that day shall Egypt be like unto women: and it shall be afraid and fear because of the shaking of the hand of the LORD of hosts, which he shaketh over it (Isa. 19:14—16).

We have seen the "perverse spirit" in the midst of Egypt, expressed by occult worship practices.

Unemployment is a vast problem in that under-developed and overpopulated nation. And the fear felt at the shaking of the hand of the Lord of Hosts is explained in the next verse. God will use Israel as the hand He shakes over Egypt, as He has done previously in the Bible. It is sometimes forgotten in this age of Jewish persecution that Israel was once mighty, and that those pagans who rose against her were severely punished. If the Canaanites had survived Joshua, or if the Philistines had survived the armies of King David, or if Antiochus and his hordes who raided Jerusalem in 167 B.C. had survived the Maccabees, any one of those could witness that Israel, with God, is a terrible force. Russia will yet see the might of God through Israel!

Israel, in her own right, is not capable of terrifying the Egyptians; rather, the Israelis are powerful "because of the counsel of the Lord of hosts." The Egyptians, as we saw, seek counsel with familiar spirits and wizards, while Israelis seek counsel with Almighty God. It is surely no contest.

And the land of Judah shall be a terror unto Egypt, every one that maketh mention thereof shall be afraid in himself, because of the counsel of the LORD of hosts, which he hath determined against it. In that day shall five cities in the land of Egypt speak the language of Canaan, and swear to the LORD of hosts; one shall be called, The city of destruction (Isa. 19:17,18).

In regard to the five Egyptian cities speaking "the language of Canaan," this apparently refers to a future occupation of Egypt by Israel.

Perhaps Egypt's internal strife and potential civil war will allow Israel to invade that land and occupy five citadels—and thus control Egypt.

But then, as matters stand today, Israel already occupies the territory of Egypt—particularly if we define Israel by her stated biblical boundaries. It was foretold that Israel would encompass an enormous amount of land:

In the same day the LORD made a covenant with Abram, saying, Unto thy seed have I given this land, from the river of Egypt unto the great river, the river Euphrates (Gen. 15:18).

But Egypt feels that the Sinai—the stretch of land that extends from present Israel to the river of Egypt—belongs to her. There are at least five settlements established in the Sinai by the Israelis, where Hebrew, "the language of Canaan," is certainly spoken.

Isaiah's language, however, suggests something more definitive, for one is hard put to find "the city of destruction" in the Sinai today. Conceivably, we will yet see Israel occupy territory in what we now regard as Egypt proper. This does not seem so startling anymore, in light of the fact that Israel has already occupied territory belonging to Jordan and to Syria. This was, of course, not the result of expansionist policies by Israel, but rather the outcome of ill-fated invasions by her enemies. Had there been peace in the Middle East ever since 1948, Israel would not have occupied cities of any foreign land.

At this point the prophet's tone changes drastically. The rest of Isaiah 19 is triumphant and unexpectedly details the true worship of the God of heaven by the Egyptians:

In that day shall there be an altar to the LORD in the midst of the land of Egypt, and a pillar at the border thereof to the LORD. And it shall be for a sign and for a witness unto the LORD of hosts in the land of Egypt: for they shall cry unto the LORD because of the oppressors, and he shall send them a saviour, and a great one, and he shall deliver them. And the LORD shall be known to Egypt, and the Egyptians shall know the LORD in that day, and shall do sacrifice and oblation; yea, they shall vow a vow unto the LORD, and perform it. And the LORD shall smite Egypt: he shall smite and heal it: and they shall return even to the LORD, and he shall be intreated of them, and shall heal them (Isa. 19:19—22).

Would anyone today expect the nation of Egypt to call upon Jehovah, the God of Israel? Actually, that righteous action also has a biblical precedent.

The city of Nineveh, including their king, repented in sackcloth and ashes in response to the prophetic message of the reluctant Jonah. Earlier in Jonah's story, the merchant seamen of Phoenicia, panicking in their floundering ship, entreated the true God and were spared.

Returning to the beginning of Israeli-Egyptian relations, the Pharaoh who confronted the dream interpretations of the astute Joseph was not above heeding the word of the Lord in regard to the approaching seven years of famine. That Pharaoh, surrounded by sun worshippers and the inevitable familiar spirits and wizards of Egypt, made the intelligent move of appointing Joseph second in command and embarking upon a rationing program to conserve his grain. He profited well by turning to Almighty God.

And so, like that ancient Pharaoh, in final desperation Egypt will turn to God Almighty. It should be said that Egypt is one of those nations that survives in the kingdom to come. Zechariah singled her out by name in referring to the worship of the Lord in that great age:

And it shall come to pass, that every one that is left of all the nations which came against Jerusalem shall even go up from year to year to worship the King, the LORD of hosts, and to keep the feast of tabernacles. And it shall be, that whoso will not come up of all the families of the earth unto Jerusalem to worship the King, the LORD of hosts, even upon them shall be no rain. And if the family of Egypt go not up, and come not, that have no rain; there shall be the plague, wherewith the LORD will smite the heathen that come not up to keep the feast of tabernacles. This shall be the punishment of Egypt, and the punishment of all nations that come not up to keep the feast of tabernacles (Zech. 14:16—19).

Egypt is actually not praised here, but used as the example of the fate for those who disregard the worship law of the kingdom. Nevertheless, that land is mentioned, and we have it as fact from Scripture that Egypt will become a part of the kingdom, which is more than can be said for many nations. For instance, in view of the prophecy, the nation of Russia will probably not be in evidence in that millennium to come.

And so, if Egypt is to survive into the kingdom, her citizens at some *previous* point must turn to the true worship of the true God: "And He shall send them a Saviour." Jesus Christ will save the Egyptians, as He saves all Israel, upon His return (Rom. 11:26).

We are seeing a degree of Christian revival in Egypt today—though not enough to justify these kingdom prophecies, of course—and the future will hold still more. Jehovah becomes angry with people, His chosen people and other nations as well. But He is also merciful and longsuffering. He will deliver Egypt and (as we shall see from the following passage) Assyria as well.

Isaiah continues with those triumphant three verses quoted in an earlier context:

In that day shall there be a highway out of Egypt to Assyria, and the Assyrian shall come into Egypt, and the Egyptian into Assyria, and the Egyptians shall serve with the Assyrians. In that day shall Israel be the third with Egypt and with Assyria, even a blessing in the midst of the land. Whom the LORD of hosts shall bless, saying, Blessed be Egypt my people, and Assyria the work of my hands, and Israel mine inheritance (Isa. 19:23—25).

How happy an ending! God calls Egypt "my people"; Assyria will become "the work of my hands"; and Israel, as always, is "mine inheritance." The three nations will be as one brotherhood in the Lord!

The highway that will connect Syria, Israel, and Egypt in a north-south direction has already been proposed by Israel. In 1971, Israel announced a highway system connecting its farflung northern and southern borders which, in effect, would connect Syria and Egypt through the occupied territories. A real highway, in the sense of a peacetime open-border policy, does not exist now, but here again is one of those shadows of the future. Naturally, there will be no need for border stations, passport checks, and the like in the presence of the Prince of Peace. When the Lord reigns in Jerusalem, the three uneasy neighbors of today's Middle East will be composed of loving believers.

What can we conclude from Isaiah 19? Perhaps "the burden of Egypt" is simply this: The nation has gone in the opposite direction from God for thousands of years, but God still awaits her citizens. Egypt is a type, a symbol of every one of us. Pagan in our ways from our very birth, each of us travels with the familiar spirits and wizards of this world and often only comes to repentance when the chips are really down.

The history and future of Egypt, as explained by the prophet Isaiah, represent a word to the wise for the unbeliever. As we watch all these things come to pass, we can only realize that salvation is as free for each of us as it will be for troubled Egypt.

The message of Isaiah 19 is the message of the Bible: However many our troubles, however many wizards lead us astray, however many Aswan Dams we build in our lifetimes, however weak and afraid we become, the Lord of Hosts still loves us. We are all, in the final analysis, "Egypt my people, and Assyria the work of my hands, and Israel mine inheritance."

EPILOGUE

At the conclusion of the sermon Pharaoh In the Promised Land, *evangelist Sutton added many notes to his foregoing analysis of the Middle East situation. As an epilogue to these four chapters we reproduce here his words following his request for the congregation to stand and pray.*

With an era of peace in the making and the Holy Spirit at work on the scale He is working, I tell you we don't have very long. Somebody asked me only recently, "Hilton, how long? Five years? Three years?" Maybe more; maybe less. I really don't know. What I do know is that the leadership of Saudi Arabia and Jordan could swing their support to Sadat tomorrow, and apply such pressure on

Assad of Syria that he would have no choice but to come along and join them.

There is an indication in Isaiah 17 that Syria could extend her opposition and get into serious trouble. In verse 1 it says the city of Damascus shall lie in ruin and be a city no more. Damascus is the capital of Syria, which is the strongest country in opposition to peace and to Sadat. We are also told in Isaiah 35 that the glory of Lebanon shall be given unto Israel. In Isaiah 19 we are told that Israel will invade Egypt and control all the major cities for a period of time in order to put down a civil war that breaks out in Egypt.

The destruction of Damascus, the capture of all southern Syria and Lebanon by Israel, and an explosion of civil strife in Egypt demanding the presence of Israeli armies in great force are as close as one bullet aimed at the head of Anwar Sadat. Do you realize that if it were possible to assassinate Mr. Sadat, it would throw Egypt into a tremendous civil war? Minority forces would move quickly to try to take over. It would certainly have originated from the PLO in southern Lebanon, supported by various Arab factors, and it would trigger a military move by Israel like you have never seen before!

You see, it has only been four months since Menachem Begin declared, "We are ready for a war of annihilation. We are prepared and can carry out a twenty-one-day war against our Arab neighbors that will annihilate them to such extent that it would be at least twenty years before they could ever mount any kind of opposition to us again."

The Israeli army is now the fifth most powerful on earth. They have the combined power of Britain and France. Israel today is a bristling arsenal—everywhere you go that's exactly what you see. Yet they have said, "We want peace!" and they have indicated how much they want peace by their willingness to return the Sinai to Egypt and to come to a compromise concerning the west bank of the River Jordan.

All these things set the stage for the final thrust of the church—which sets the stage for the appearing of Jesus!

5

THE CAMP DAVID CONNECTION

What a difficult thing it is to write a commentary on prophecy these days! What are the authors to do when prophecies are fulfilled even as they write about them?

The original version of this book was to have ended with the epilogue preceding this chapter. The message given by Reverend Sutton concerning the peace initiative shown by President Sadat and Prime Minister Begin was to have been detailed and explained with reference to the Tribulation period prophecies covered earlier. But now, before going to press, we find still further events on the world political scene offering themselves for our scrutiny. Thus new material is needed and more commentary is appropriate. The Camp David meeting and all of its far-reaching consequences cannot be ignored in a book of this kind. Wherever possible, we must seek the answers to these new developments.

Scripture is brief and to the point: Men are garrulous, quarrelsome, and tediously lengthy about their negotiations. Lest we miss some vital point pertaining to the fulfillment of prophecy, we now review in detail the remarkable conference at Camp David.

The Cast of Characters

We have thoroughly reviewed the leading participants in the Camp David conference. We have seen the unlikelihood of a meeting of the minds among these three national leaders, who certainly make odd political bedfellows. We have wondered at the positive nature of their communication under the circumstances, and we have cited this very communication as an act of God.

And if it seemed unlikely that Carter, Begin, and Sadat could communicate in a way so advantageous for peace at a distance, we must be awed that they could do so face to face. Many noted political commentators gave Camp David little chance of success.

Surely Jimmy Carter, a farmer from Georgia, could not have the wherewithal to bring together the archenemies of the Middle East. Surely President Sadat would not commit himself to any drastic solutions on American soil. And Prime Minister Begin could not be expected to give anything away in a secret conclave held so far from the Promised Land. News coverage was minimal, at the request of the conferees.

The three national leaders each put a lot on the line at Camp David. President Carter was suffering a sharp decline in his national political image, and a failure at that particular conference could have spelled his demise as a political figure. Commentators believed he would sign his own political death warrant if he reached an inconclusive result, revealing himself to be a weakling at international politics. The president's own staff seemed nervous at the prospects.

Carter had chosen an inordinately difficult forum at which to manifest his negotiating skills. At such a juncture in his political career, one might have expected Carter to take on something simpler. Tax cuts, inflation-fighting measures, or the like might have granted him a better chance at significant political gains than this stubborn Middle Eastern peace situation. Nevertheless, Carter chose to place his political life on the line in search for an answer to the problems in God's central theatre of operations.

President Sadat's position was yet more drastic. Should he fail at that meeting he would come under serious attack from his Arab detractors. His momentous visit to Jerusalem had certainly won him no popularity, and further conferences only created increasing antagonism among his unfriendly Arab neighbors. Sadat had lost some favor even among the populace of Egypt, and it appeared that a failure at Camp David might cause his ultimate fall. There was also a grim possibility of open war with Israel. Egypt could not have survived another declared war, and Sadat's leadership of his nation would surely have come to an end.

Prime Minister Begin also came to Camp David with much to lose. He was already in political trouble at home, with diverse factions of Israel lining up against his policies. While the majority of Israelis certainly wanted a just peace, many were nervous about the concessions the prime minister might have to make. Certainly the hard-won settlements in the occupied territories must be preserved. But what of Egypt's demand that all that land be returned? A failure on Begin's part to advance the peace initiative would have set the stage for a fifth military clash with the Arabs. Although militarily strong, Israel is still an underdog in terms of numbers and cannot even afford to *win* such wars. The casualty rates among the relative handful of Israelis in each of the previous wars are simply too heavy for that nation to bear. Under no circumstances could another war be risked. Furthermore, each war had become more difficult than the one before it. Israel's memory of the infamous Yom Kippur War of 1973 was keen, and the nation would not tolerate another debacle. Begin's political career would end if the aging revolutionary failed to find the right formula for peace.

The prime minister also faced pressure from factions within the Carter administration. Certain officials would have liked to unseat the hard-driving prime minister of Israel in order to deal with a less intractable successor. Surely a man who had blown up buildings and hunted down occupying troops in his youth was not one to discuss peace with. Facing political pressures in Israel and America as well, Begin still chose to come to Camp David.

Do Or Die

The Camp David summit had a "do or die" feeling about it. If it had collapsed or been inconclusive, peace in the Middle East would have been seriously threatened. The world awaited the outcome, watching daily for any morsel of news from an almost silent press corps. The security surrounding those meetings added to their mystery. No news went in or out of Camp David; desperate newsmen trying for a scoop were always stopped by the formidable security forces as the "Big Three" met within. The idyllic atmosphere of those cool forests contrasted strongly with the import of those heated conversations.

When the summit did not fold within five days, everyone knew agreements would be forthcoming. What was not known, of course, was how far-reaching the peace plan would be, or whether the parties would *truly* be in agreement. But the conference survived its initial talks and the world waited for further developments.

Finally the delegates came forth, and with reasonably good news. There was a definite warmth between the parties, and in particular the atmosphere of friendship established in November of 1977 between Sadat and Begin seemed to remain intact. Both men praised Carter for his tactful and determined efforts toward peace.

Perhaps we were spared the catastrophe of the leaders walking out on each other, denouncing one another, or leaving the conference prematurely. On the other hand, no peace treaty was signed either.

In substance, general terms were agreed upon. Israel would withdraw from occupied territory, and Egypt would grant peace between the two nations. But in a few days much discussion ensued over just what territories Israel would return and when. The two Middle Eastern leaders returned home to face both displeasure and praise. They shared the Nobel Peace Prize even as they debated furiously with opposition parties in their respective governments.

Camp David furthered the peace ideal. The essence of Mr. Sadat's proposal of November, 1977, was preserved; the two nations would find their way to peace. But certain details, ominously important, remained to be worked out. A step had been made in the direction of peace, but further steps would be necessary.

If Camp David were indeed a "do or die" event, then the world had managed to stay on the less deadly path.

Step By Step

The painstaking progress toward peace that we are now witnessing in world affairs is implicit in the prophecies of Ezekiel. We have reviewed that prophet's forecasts of situations leading to the

Russian invasion of Israel. We may now see that the step-by-step peace process is implied in Ezekiel 38:8,11,14. First Israel is regathered; then they "dwell safely" and are "at rest"; finally we come to the actual invasion.

Perhaps we are now seeing Israel dwelling safely (relative to her past, of course), and maybe when a more complete peace covenant is formed we can fairly call her "at rest." All this time, if we read the prophets correctly, the invader to the north watches carefully.

The reunion of Esau and Jacob, which we reviewed in the course of studying the relationship of Sadat and Begin, also has a step-by-step recounting in the Scriptures (Gen. 32,33). In the course of that historic reunion, Jacob bowed to the ground seven times before Esau. Will we observe seven distinct acts in the overall peace negotiations between Sadat and Begin? After all, a just and lasting peace will have to include the major Arab nations along with Egypt. The present reunion of Israel and Egypt is one phase in the process, and others may follow. In a sense, the two brother nations have bowed themselves twice: once in November, 1977, and again at Camp David. But a complete and thorough peace will require much more "bowing."

A true peace would involve the policies of other nations too. Prime Minister Begin's analysis of the situation is quite accurate. Begin stated, "Peace with Egypt makes it impossible for Syria to make war with Israel, as it would be sheer suicide for them; Jordan cannot make war, for to do so would certainly cause King Hussein to lose his crown."

Indeed, it seems that neither of Israel's border enemies to the north or east feels secure in attacking Israel singly or in concert without a simultaneous attack from Egypt. Syria and Jordan, heavily outnumbering Israel, are still respectful of her might—or at least they have seen the historical vengeance of the God of Israel on the battlefield. We conclude from the prophecies that even mighty Russia is loathe to attack Israel without a full conclave of local allies in the fighting arena.

As we work out the further steps and try to predict the actions of nations, we become highly speculative. It would seem that the pressure of world opinion would fall heavily on the Arab nations to make peace with Israel if Egypt does so. Undoubtedly there will be a few holdouts, however, and these will tend to migrate toward closer ties with Russia.

From Ezekiel's prophecies it is clear that Libya and Iraq will be holdouts and will finally ally themselves with Israel's far northern enemy (Ezek. 38:5). Iraq comes into the scene as a part of the former Persian Empire. Ezekiel's actual naming of the allies in the invasion is certainly a convenience to us, since the nations survive and their animosity toward Israel is very obvious at this time.

Iran, comprising the major geographical area of the former Persian Empire, is ever an enigma. The shah either supported the Israelis or took a noncommital posture throughout the thirty years of his rule. As a matter of fact, it was the nonparticipation of Iran in the enemy circle that caused many to doubt the accuracy of Ezekiel's forecast. If the prophet had mentioned Persia, and Persia refused to take a stand against Israel, then either Ezekiel's foresight was cloudy or it was not time for his prophecies to be fulfilled.

But on March 6, 1978, the shah announced he was changing his posture toward Israel. The monarch declared a position of opposition toward the Holy Land, which changed the balance of power in the Middle East. It also seemed to cause enormous trouble for the shah. After the shah's announcement, his nation was plagued with riots, demonstrations, and social upheaval. One is reminded of the terrible visitations upon the palace of Pharaoh in the days when Abraham and Sarah visited Egypt, and again when Moses pleaded for the freedom of the children of Israel. The principle was established clearly in Genesis 12:3; God will curse those who curse Abraham's seed.

It is interesting that it is the presence of the pagans and their ferocity in the land of the shah that brought about troubles similar to those caused by Pharaoh's magicians and wizards. The ancient Moslem rites were threatened by the shah's eagerness to take his nation into twentieth-century technological achievement.

We might compare the present troubles of Iran with those already experienced by the nation of England. We cited earlier the fundamental change in British-Israeli relations during the return of the Jews to the Promised Land in 1947—48. We have seen how the English changed from support of the Jews through the Balfour Agreement to their later opposition; this change in policy led to considerable suffering on the part of the beleaguered British people. This example gives us the validity of hindsight. Is Iran following the same hazardous course in its relations with Israel?

Even Russia, as we have seen, has followed a similar course of action in her relations with Israel. She first welcomed the "new" nation into the United Nations in 1948 and made certain gestures of courtship, Russian-style; but just as quickly she turned against the Promised Land and, as we have seen from the prophecies, will inevitably pay the price.

America's Choice

Our own nation has thus far avoided the dangerous policy of antagonism. America, host of the Camp David conference and initiator of the original peace talks, has remained Israel's steadfast ally, unlike England, Russia, and now Iran (and others who also could be named, reaching back into history even to Abraham), who have come under the curse of Genesis 12:3. But that verse also contains a blessing, and the United States has been abundantly blessed.

In spite of our wickedness, violence, and corruption, we have not mistreated the Jewish people nor left the side of our allies in the Promised Land. God's blessings on our nation are as certain as His curses upon others. The blessings of God on the American people are manifold, and we can count on them so long as we continue to stand by the Jews.

The Jew has found a real home in America for two centuries now. In no other nation in the long,

long history of Israel have the Jewish people been able to lead lives free of fear, prejudice, and anti-Semitism. The chosen people have paid a terrible toll in many nations, but America has not exacted tribute from this oppressed people. God has kept His end of the bargain, and our country stands secure today, determining to be, if necessary, Israel's only ally.

But while we are collecting our blessings by supporting Israel, we also must prove ourselves a friend to the Arab nations—and this is no easy task. Diplomacy of the highest order is required for America to pursue amicable relationships with nations opposed to Israel's presence in the Middle East. We have had to grant military, industrial, and financial aid to Arab nations as well as to Israel, in order to bring about this delicate balance of peace in the Middle East. Our conciliation is like approaching a feuding family and trying to pacify all members in the attempt to join them together.

In aiding the Arabs we are aiding the descendants of Abraham through Ishmael. If we are able to accomplish this difficult task, we may be able to bring many years of peaceful relations to that potentially explosive part of the world.

6

PEACE?

We are now living in such an intense age of prophecy fulfillment that it is becoming impossible to chronicle the onrushing events in a book. A book takes at least a matter of months to write and print and distribute, and we are experiencing a certain frustration by merely trying to keep up with the oncoming acts of God. Even as we write we are falling behind.

The discerning reader will see that since the time of writing the earlier portions of this book, certain elements of the final picture have been fulfilled. In our first chapter we were weighing the chances of a true peace treaty emerging from the visit of Pharaoh to the Promised Land. In this final chapter, written some months later, that peace treaty has been accomplished. We would certainly be remiss not to include an analysis of the treaty and its effects in this book, and so we must, in effect, include material that we had no idea was forthcoming.

At some point, of course, this book must end. We plan this to be the final chapter unless the Russian invasion of Israel and the Tribulation period should overtake us before we are finished! (If the reader gets the feeling that the end times are virtually upon us, then he will not have missed the point of this book.)

Ezekiel Lives!

How truly remarkable it is that a 2,500-year-old prophecy is literally being fulfilled month by month as we work. Those who were exiled in Babylon and heard the original lessons of the patient Ezekiel looked forward misty-eyed to our time. The heavily burdened Ezekiel, teacher of an enslaved people, dutifully proclaimed the word of God in Babylon. The remnant people of Judah heard of still another invasion, and finally, lasting peace.

How they must have speculated on what the prophet meant! When he reported his vision of the valley of dry bones (Ezek. 37) did they picture an early restoration to Jerusalem or did they apprehend his greater meaning—that a worldwide dispersion would someday conclude with a magnificent restoration of the chosen people to their Promised Land, as in A.D. 1948?

Did they fear an immediate invasion from the north as soon as they returned to reoccupy

Jerusalem and rebuild their temple? What was their interpretation of Magog and all those other tribal names they may not have recognized in their times? We must appreciate that written versions of the prophecies were few and far between— particularly in a hostile enemy's territory—and Ezekiel's followers may not have understood his geographical symbols. Perhaps they didn't know what to make of the arcane prophet's mystical visions and overwhelmingly dramatic picture of things to come. Scripture indicates that Ezekiel was considered a little unbalanced, perhaps even raving, and it is likely that he was taken seriously by only a few.

But now 2,500 years have passed, and *we are seeing what they heard!*

Outdated Books

The Bible is the only reliable book of prophecy, and the only one which will never go out of date.

Actually, books on prophecy by earthly authors are in a sense a bad buy. They may be perfectly accurate to the degree that they correctly present the Scriptures. The problem is that they are written in the world of time, and in these days they go out of date all too quickly. Such a classic as Hal Lindsey's *The Late Great Planet Earth*, while biblically accurate to date, is "out of fashion" because it was written over ten years ago. Wars have come and gone, nations have changed alliances, treaties have been signed, and governments have toppled since Hal Lindsey presented his analyses of prophecy. *The Late Great Planet Earth* is certainly still a magnificent book and a one-of-a-kind witness to the unbelieving world; but because of the acts of God that have transpired since its publication, it is no longer up to date.

Ten years is a short time. Mr. Lindsey undertook to explain prophecies that went back to the book of Genesis! Nothing in *The Late Great Planet Earth* has been found incorrect; it's just that the almighty God is moving so fast today that the book has passed its era!

A similar fate has befallen *The Coming Russian Invasion of Israel* by Zola Levitt and Thomas S. McCall. That book, too, has become outdated by world events, and it was written *six* years ago! Since that 1973 writting, three nations have reversed their positions toward Israel and a newer book of prophecy is again needed.

The Coming Russian Invasion of Israel analyzed that prophecy in all of its myriad details, but at the time it was written Egypt, Ethiopia, and Iran all had different positions toward Israel than they now do. The authors were able to speculate that Egypt would become inactive in any hostile way toward Israel, but fell short of actually predicting a peace treaty. Leaving the prophecy to the prophets, the authors were able to say only that Egypt would be "neutralized" by the time of the Russian invasion, since that country was not listed as one of Russia's allies.

They also were forced to note that both Ethiopia and Iran held non-hostile positions toward Israel at the time of writing. There would have been no way for the authors to have foreseen that those two nations—both listed as allies of Russia in the coming invasion—would so radically change their views. They couldn't have known that Ethiopia's Emperor Haile Selassie would be toppled by a military regime that became Marxist immediately and expressed great animosity toward the Promised Land.

Selassie, the former emperor, liked to think of himself as "The Lion of the Tribe of Judah," fancifully tracing his heritage back to a supposed liaison between King Solomon and the Queen of Sheba. He was at worst neutral and to some degree pro-Israel, since he enjoyed in his own estimation a "biblical lineage." Without question, times have changed in Ethiopia. The new government is the publicly sworn enemy of Israel, and would gladly join Russia or anyone else in an invasion of the Promised Land.

With Iran, of course, the picture has grown very bleak where Israel is concerned. The shah, for all his questionable policies, was never a real enemy of Israel. He supplied oil to that nation and maintained a hands-off policy where Middle Eastern conflicts were concerned. He was at least neutral toward Israel and was clearly anti-Communist. But on March 6, 1978, he publicly announced a change of attitude. He had gravitated away from Israel and toward the PLO.

It is notable that his opposition escalated immediately, as foreseen by Genesis 12:3: "I will curse him that curseth thee [Israel]". It seemed that from that date onward the shah's hold on his own government became tenuous, and we have now witnessed his complete overthrow.

As matters now stand in Iran, the Islamic government is passionately anti-Israel, and PLO leader Yasser Arafat has taken advantage of that situation. A picture published internationally showed Iran's Khomeini kissing Arafat in the traditional Islamic gesture of brotherhood. This bodes fearsome consequences for Israel. Iran, listed by Ezekiel as one of the allies of Russia in the invasion, has now taken her place as expected.

For those who do not read Ezekiel it must have seemed surprising that so powerful a figure as Shah Mohammad Reza Pahlavi, with the support of his 430,000-man American-equipped army and air force, was defeated by a disorganized group of religious zealots and leftist workers. But the student of prophecy could hardly be surprised.

The Russians are taking immediate advantage, of course; reports of "refugees" from Afghanistan slipping over the border into Iran represent the next logical step. The so-called refugees must surely be the Communist organizers who, like perpetual funeral guests, always attend the demise of a government. They will rally the already leftist forces to wrest the government of Iran from its religious leadership, and the predicted alliance will get underway. We are now risking a few speculations, of course, but if the scenario follows the standard Russian techniques of the past—in Eastern Europe and lately in Africa—we can soon color Iran Red.

This book has indeed become dated during the writing. Chapter 1 speculates on what happens in Chapter 6, and will probably be further outdated as the readers receive it. Realize that this is a *new* book, being printed as fast as a distinguished publishing house can work. Those in the editorial offices, comprehending as they do the messages of prophecy in the Bible, are aware that the very work they are doing may well be outdistanced by the plan of God.

Well and good. "Amen. Even so, come, Lord Jesus."

"Peace: Risks and Rewards"

In the March 26, 1979, issue of *Time* magazine was a lengthy story called "Peace: Risks and Rewards." The *Time* writers, oblivious as they invariably are of biblical prophecy, attempted to evaluate the remarkable peace treaty orchestrated by President Carter (and paid for by the American people, as some readers of *Time* would have it in the letter column). *Time* wrestled with the heavy questions. What would be the situation in Egypt when things really came to a head and President Sadat had to face his international Arab cousins? What would be the reaction in Jerusalem to returning the territory in the Sinai? Why was the reaction of both Israel and Egypt to the signing of a peace covenant the immediate purchase of billions of dollars' worth of weapons? What would happen next in this confounding labyrinth of the Middle East, with its wars, its oil, its impassioned populations, its religions, and its 5,000-year history of dread unrest? It was well beyond the scope of a weekly news magazine, whose articles only serve to hawk the products of its advertisers, to make a sensible analysis of all that is happening.

The *reactions* to the article were more notable

than the content of the article itself. There was a sour response on the part of many letter writers who confused temporal gains with the will of God. Their view can be summed up in one letter that appeared in the April 23, 1979, issue:

Your story "Peace: Risks and Rewards" was notable for its failure to mention any rewards for Americans. Will this peace between Israel and Egypt better our relations with the U.S.S.R. or decelerate Moscow's growing influence over its neighbors, increase our access to energy sources, reduce our rate of inflation, improve our balance of payments, help balance our budget, or increase our national security?

While the unbelievers of America count their money, court false friends like the Communists, and worry over their own comforts, three million Jews stand with their backs to the wall. Even without the biblical implications, couldn't we be somewhat less materialistic and self-centered when a sister democracy is threatened? Could we not show a little compassion for a beleaguered people whose enemies can be counted in the hundred millions? Could we not grant that the Israelis have built a nation in thirty years that rivals the best we know?

The position of the American believers is much different, of course. The true church realizes the full implications of the peace treaty, and we look from that realization to the imminent coming of *true* peace. The point of view from the Bible is so different from that of *Time* magazine that we seem to be looking at events of different planets.

Nearly six years have passed since the Yom Kippur War of 1973. We have seen three American presidents earnestly pursue peace in the Middle East, and we have finally seen all these actions and efforts pay off. The first treaty has been signed and Israel and Egypt are technically at peace. But our newsmen have asked, "For how long?" Can Egypt survive the Arab pressure? Will the other Arab countries follow Egypt's example, or will they bolt and cause severe problems?

The Bible has answers, as usual. The peace with Egypt will last, and it should become part of a chain reaction that will eventually pressure Israel's other Arab neighbors to make peace. If we can rely on Ezekiel's description of Israel at peace and rest (Ezek. 38:8,11,14), we assume that the prophet indicates a complete settling of all existing differences. Strong attempts will probably be made to destroy that peace, but apparently these attempts will fail. After all, the Arabs are hardly united, and Egypt, a large and relatively strong nation, can survive the pressure brought to bear on her. The United States can be counted on to aid Egypt in this difficult time, and even Israel may begin assisting the troubled Egyptians.

President Sadat stands in a dangerous position as a result of his initiatives toward peace. The PLO has announced that the death or overthrow of Sadat would not overly upset their organization, hoping the Egyptian people might take this matter into their own hands. President Sadat is beginning to have as many enemies as Israel itself. If Sadat is assassinated or overthrown by some pro-PLO regime, Egypt would probably be propelled into terrible internal strife. Would this be the fulfillment of Isaiah's picture of Egyptians fighting Egyptians?

And I will set the Egyptians against the Egyptians: and they shall fight every one against his brother, and every one against his neighbour; city against city, and kingdom against kingdom (Isa. 19:2).

Will the government of Egypt fall into evil hands?

And the spirit of Egypt shall fail in the midst thereof; and I will destroy the counsel thereof: and they shall seek to the idols, and to the charmers, and to them that have familiar spirits, and to the wizards (Isa. 19:3).

Isaiah goes on to point out that Judah "shall be a terror unto Egypt" (establishing the existence of Israel at the time of Egypt's civil war). The language of Judah will be spoken in Egypt (Isa. 19:18). Suppose civil war breaks out in Egypt in answer to the death or overthrow of President Sadat, and Israeli intervention is required for settlement. Before the peace treaty we certainly could not have expected Israel to be concerned over internal Egyptian matters, but the treaty changes everything. Israel will be moved to help those who would oppose that new regime and who hold to the treaty terms. Conceivably, Israeli armed forces would occupy certain cities of Egypt until stability could be reestablished.

We are again speculating on the terms of Isaiah's prophecy, but we have every hope that our book will not be outdated too quickly. After all, as prophetic events come to pass we can see ahead that much more clearly. Any students of prophecy today could enlighten those listeners of Ezekiel and Isaiah just through our advantage of seeing the events of our day come to pass.

The Burden of Damascus

Isaiah had more to say about the Middle East than just chapter 19. The first verse of chapter 17 is overwhelmingly tragic:

The burden of Damascus. Behold, Damascus is taken away from being a city, and it shall be a ruinous heap. (Isa. 17:1).

We know this prophecy is for the future because Damascus has never been so devastated; indeed, it still stands as the capital of Syria. It was attacked time and again in biblical days, but it remains. The closest it has come to utter destruction was in 1967 and 1973, when exasperated and determined Israeli land armies nearly occupied the Syrian capital.

But Isaiah envisions "a ruinous heap." Can this statement of prophecy fit into the present scenario?

With apologies again for speculating, we see three possible destinies for Damascus. Possibly Syria will ally with Iraq as is now planned, and militarily oppose the Middle East peace treaty. This sort of action might cause Israel to take an offensive stance and throw swift and powerful blows at her northern neighbor. Damascus by its proximity would become an early target.

Or perhaps Syria will join in the present peace movement and become the temporary friend of Israel for her own purposes. However, the moment Russia attacks, Syria could—and probably would—take sides with the invaders. Syrian territory would be at the disposal of the forces from the north; as we know from prophecy, those forces will be crushed as they reach Israel's northern border. In such devastation as God promises upon Gog and Magog (Ezek. 38:18—23), Damascus would certainly suffer.

Still another version of the demise of Damascus would be in the final culmination of all wars, the fearful Armageddon. With its nearness to the Valley of Megiddo and the enormity of the mobilized armies of the whole earth, Damascus wouldn't have a chance.

Although it has stood for thousands upon thousands of years, Damascus is doomed.

The Treaty

We could go on through prophecy, finding the destinies of the various nations now occupied by the Arab peoples. As we speculate on *how* these destinies will come about, we might be right in some cases and wrong in others. But we can safely evaluate the peace treaty between Israel and Egypt, and its implications for the future, based on its terms as we now understand them.

How intriguing that one part of our book has in

a way, already been justified. Earlier we compared the meeting of Begin and Sadat to the reunion of Jacob and Esau in Genesis 32 and 33. We can now add a detail that strengthens this analogy.

Prime Minister Begin and the Knesset have agreed to return lands in the Sinai to Egypt as part of the terms of the new peace agreement. The same principle is established in the story of Jacob and Esau. Jacob, whose seed was chosen by God to enjoy the inheritance of the covenant, relinquished much of his inheritance to Esau in order to bring about peace between him and his brother. Esau even objected to the generosity of his brother: "And Esau said, I have enough, my brother; keep that thou hast unto thyself" (Gen. 33:9).

But Jacob, forefather of modern Israel, persisted for the sake of a just peace:

And Jacob said, Nay, I pray thee, if now I have found grace in thy sight, then receive my present at my hand: for therefore I have seen thy face, as though I had seen the face of God, and thou wast pleased with me. Take, I pray thee, my blessing that is brought to thee; because God hath dealt graciously with me, and because I have enough. And he urged him, and he took it (Gen. 33:10,11).

The two were made brothers again in the manner of Begin and Sadat. The rightfully covenanted one returned that which was his by divine will in order to achieve peaceful relations, and we have now seen the process repeated.

As to the other terms of the treaty, they are typical. Diplomatic relations will be established, along with free movement of citizens across the borders and equitable trade. Both sides are disconcertingly armed to the teeth, presumably to scare off external enemies, but for the moment the treaty looks successful. We can finish our book in the hope that nothing shocking will put it out of date before it is published.

But know this—the peace treaty is by no means the end of hostilities in the Middle East!

The Rest of the Story

True peace will not come to this world until the Prince of Peace brings it, and that's all there is to that.

This peace treaty is a stopgap measure. Indeed, its success will be in keeping Egypt out of the hostilities of the Russian invasion of Israel, and perhaps bringing about some interesting prophecy fulfillments of its own (Isa. 19, etc.). But the *ultimate* peace treaty with Israel still waits to be signed.

The Antichrist will step forward and make his covenant with Israel (Dan. 9:27), violate it (1 Thess. 2:3,4), and proceed to initiate the battle of Armageddon. Egypt and everyone else will be involved, since the only place to hide from Armageddon will be heaven. Only the church, the bride of Christ, will be safe from that ultimate disaster. The world below will be devastated.

The King will then come and establish true peace on earth and goodwill toward men, as promised. His kingdom will endure a thousand years and then all believers will proceed to eternity. We have already begun eternal life. Obviously, it is going to get better!

May we, then, end our book as the apostle John ended his: "The grace of our Lord Jesus Christ be with you all. Amen" (Rev. 22:21).